THE ANGELS OF
DECEMBER

A TRUE STORY
by
Thomas Fletcher-Michaels

Park Press Quality Printing Incorporated • P.O. Box 475 • Waite Park Minnesota 56387

Cover photo (taken at Monastic Cemetery, Sisters of the Order of St. Benedict, St. Joseph, MN) and photos in Part 2 by Thomas Fletcher-Michaels.

Some images are used by permission of Zedcor, Inc., Tucson, AZ, from the *30,000 Image Desk Gallery®️ Collection.* 1-800-482-4567.

©️ Copyright Thomas F. Michaels 1995
ISBN: 0-9652044-0-5
Printed and Published in USA by Park Press, Inc., P.O. Box 475, Waite Park, MN 56387

Correspondence to the author should be addressed to him, c/o Park Press.

I dedicate this book
to all of those
who suffered as a result
of my ignorance.
And I ask all to believe.

Acknowledgments

I thank my family for their continued support, not only during this dramatic transition in my life, but for being there for me in spite of my "shortcomings." A special thank you (sent in prayer) to the late Monsignor Vincent A. Yzermans for his encouragement and endorsement of this book. To Ed and Kay Goering I extend my gratitude and lasting friendship for their faith and advice in this project. And thanks to Shelly Ford for her unselfish gesture of trust in this book, in me and the successful completion of this project.

A special thank you to Andy Hilger for his faith in me and his belief in the positive effect of this book on others, and for his advice to meet with Jim Blommer of Park Press. I absolutely cannot say enough about the special group of people working at Park Press, the freedom and cooperation I was given on this project far exceeded what I had anticipated. A very special thank you to Jim and Dorothy Blommer for their confidence in me, and to the others who worked on this project behind the scenes to bring about the beautiful completion of this book, among them, Bob Briggs and David Kwolik. My sincere thanks to you all.

Introduction

A T A VERY YOUNG AGE I SET OUT ON my own to find the truth about the meaning of life. This was done out of necessity because I could sense little truth in what I had been told and led to believe by others. I started out on this journey alone; that was my first mistake because I had no idea where I was going. I became lost during my search many times, never believing I would ever find my way home again. This is the story of that search.

What you are about to read is a true story about the depths of despair, a life filled with drugs, alcohol, reform school, prison, physical and emotional abuse, isolation, emptiness, and hopelessness. There are many similarities between my experiences and what I perceive to be hell. The madness in my life continued for 43 years; that was the duration of my search. Then, through the grace of God, my life changed completely. It began with supernatural experiences, then God began to work in me and through me to such an extent the other guy who lived in this body was gone.

There is not one area of my life which has not been affected. The changes actually began overnight three years ago on December 1, 1991. The intensity and depth of these experiences has not decreased, it has actually increased to a point where I feel as though my life has been saturated by the Spirit of God.

As I was growing up, absorbing the feelings I sensed in those around me, I thought there might be a God. But the experiences I have had in the past three years and the effects of those experiences have removed all doubt.

If you have spent a great deal of your life looking for the

answers as I have, you may want to read this book. I believe I have been given some of those answers; and I believe I have a responsibility to share them with others. I offer this testimony in all humility and with immense gratitude to God.

Thomas Fletcher-Michaels
November, 1994

Foreword
by
Ed Goering

BOUT THREE YEARS AGO MY friend Tom called me and wanted to share some startling experiences he was having. As I climbed the stairs to his apartment I recalled that in recent months he had been in and out of treatment centers because of his addiction. His life was a shambles and he was all alone and in a very deep hole, personally. As I entered his apartment I could see it was filled with plants and many images that suggested that this was the home of a spiritual person. Tom began to speak about a series of spiritual experiences he was having. I'm familiar with Alcoholics Anonymous and the stories of addicts that have "hit bottom," and finally turned to God. Some of them spoke the way Tom was now speaking. For over thirty years I've known Tom as a fellow who seemed to be on a high horse and now he seemed to be on his knees in prayer to God.

Tom came into my life over thirty years ago and he's been in and out of my life ever since. Our first meeting was when I was a young social worker fresh out of graduate school. Tom surely needed a friend. He was what we call a loner, socially isolated, one who had no true intimate relationship with anyone. He was in trouble with himself, with others and with all of life. Over the years we have met at many places—street corners, hospitals, detox centers and even in prison.

I remember telling Tom years ago that he reminded me of the perch that nibbled on my hook when I went out to catch sunfish. The perch would nibble all my bait away but never got hooked. We would talk about the things of God, and Tom would nibble, but he never got hooked either.

Tom would vanish from my life and then one day he would be back again. And again I asked him, as I had in the past many times, if he had gotten around to reading Francis Thompson's poem, "The Hound of Heaven." It seemed in a way that this was also Tom's story; God was always after Tom, but Tom was on the run. In a way Tom would glance toward Heaven and wonder a little, but then he was gone again.

During these last three years Tom has continued to share these new experiences of his life with me. More than once I remember standing back and wondering—do we have here the makings of a miracle? I recalled a time, years ago, when I was in treatment for my own addiction at a place called Hazelden in Minnesota. In one room there was a beautiful plaque made from a slice out of a tree trunk. On it were the words, "The House of Miracles." Surely, many people knew about their friends in treatment, as I have known Tom, and they would say, "If that fellow straightens out it would be a miracle."

But Tom was not just an addict, he was the kind who my friends in AA refer to as "low bottom alcoholics." A lot of guys like him don't get sober—they just get dead. Tom and I have some things in common with our addictive histories. Everything was always done totally and intensely; our negative behaviors were not luke warm. Even the anger at our creator God—blaming Him for all the suffering and pain in our lives—was done with an intensity. There is a type of common sense that if Tom was now open to God, this too would be done with an intensity.

During these three years, Tom wondered how people, who have known him over the years, could possibly believe these experiences he speaks of. I recalled, with him, the story in the Bible about Saul of Tarsus, a persecutor of Christians, who was converted by God to become the great Christian missionary, St. Paul. When St. Paul was introduced to the young Christian community as a new Christian convert and spokesman, there were those who were very reluctant to believe in or trust this fellow. They remembered his recent history, the way he had been living his life. It is easy to see someone wondering about Tom in the same way, questioning whether this new behavior of this old addict is simply the result of brain damage from excessive drug abuse—or *had* he simply, finally, gone over the edge. It's easy to understand someone finding it hard to believe that Tom was really, really touched by the hand of God, especially since his past is very tarnished. Ah, but then Jesus did say that He came to heal the sick, the sick-sinner. Tom would surely qualify!

It does seem that during these past years, Tom's life has been dramatically changing. Tom would speak with some concern about some of his character traits that were still operating in him, as if he wanted them all to be gone, wishing that struggling with his humaness was no longer necessary. We all need to know conversion is a process, a long process. I reminded Tom that after St. Paul was converted, he still had his same personality, only it was now being used to serve God. Tom is still the good hustler-con artist, but now these "skills" are to be used to serve the Lord instead of Tom.

In this book, Tom feels compelled to share with us the story, his life's story, of someone who was wounded and scared, and angry, someone trying to get even, and someone who seemed to be running away from the God who pursues all of us. Tom told me, and he is telling you, that he finally reached toward heaven and God embraced him. Tom is my friend, and I believe in him because I want to. God can work His will as He wishes, why not through Tom?

There are experiences in the life of the old and the new Tom that are uncommon to us, yet many of us can personally identify with some of both. We all are lost in our own ways and we all come to know God in our own unique ways. This is the story of one lost man who was found.

Ed Goering, M.S.W.
December, 1994

1 If our destination is unknown, we shall never arrive.

I CAN REMEMBER WHEN I WAS FOUR years old, sitting on my bedroom floor, bouncing my head against the wall in a steady and comfortable rhythm, almost as though I was resisting the physical part of myself. This is where I went to think, to meditate. It seemed there was something in me that wanted out. When it wouldn't come out, I went in after it. The spot on the wall became well worn, then the plaster fell away from the boards, and there was a circular hole through which you could see the wooden lathe behind the paint and plaster.

My room was my "in between" place. I remember there were no shadows, no light and dark, just a semi-darkness. I very seldom sat on the bed, my favorite spot was right there next to the bed on the floor. I would think and dream, and I would fall into a rhythm bouncing against the wall, eyes closed and my mind closed to this world. It had become my refuge, my place to go to withdraw from people and things, my hiding place.

I was discovering I had to live in this body and adapt to this world. I did not adapt well and found myself in constant rebellion. A part of me refused to play by the rules. As life went on, I discovered there were a lot of other people who felt the same way.

I saw people lying and cheating, whether it be in games or to cover an error, or to get something they didn't deserve. People in general didn't seem content or filled with peace; I saw chaos wherever I looked. I may have been young but there was nothing wrong with my eyes and ears. I saw more evidence of fear and anger—whether it be from my father or neighbors, or the children of

neighbors or someone in a store, a stranger—than I did of goodness, love and sharing. It seemed that everyone agreed for the most
part that love, kindness, and similar virtues were right and best.
Why then did so many people behave in such a way as to nourish
conflict in their lives? Our family life was filled with conflict which
began as a whisper and grew into screams. Where was the good
stuff? Were those things only on television? Were those values only
present in the *Ozzie and Harriet Show*, and *Father Knows Best*? It
seemed to me that reality was a whole lot different from what I
had been led to believe. Were these just my problems, or were they
everyone's? My disappointment in others seemed to be all the
justification I needed to behave the way I did. And my behavior
did not make me popular.

　　I remember when I was very young, my mother was having coffee with the neighbor lady whose son was one of my play-
mates. I went in the breezeway where they were having their coffee and told my mother the other kids wouldn't play with me.
The neighbor lady called her son in and told him he had to let me
participate in the activities as well. I remember feeling as if I were
an outsider, someone who did not belong. I felt ashamed that no
one wanted to play with me, but my behavior was usually not
appropriate. I was always looking for some mischief, to "stir
things up." I wanted to be in charge; to be the leader; but my
leadership abilities were in short supply as were my friendships
even at that young age.

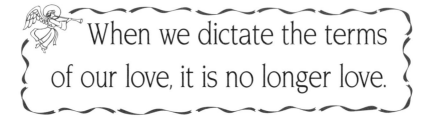

When we dictate the terms
of our love, it is no longer love.

　　My father was always very critical. That, coupled with
almost no positive input, didn't leave me feeling very confident
about myself. So I started out in life feeling as though I didn't

have any value. I had low self-esteem and I was extremely self-conscious. I was afraid I wouldn't be liked by others. Feelings like that about myself bred additional negative feelings. It was as though I started out in life with three strikes against me. I remember feelings of isolation as early as four years old. The beginning of my life had such a weak foundation, I found it very hard to build anything permanent. My values and priorities became ever-changing. I'm sure my out-

My first haircut, at age three.

rageous behavior was an attempt to get attention. While it did get me the attention I sought, the consequences of my actions generally lowered my self-esteem even further; and, in effect, alienated me from others.

I can't remember the first time I stole something, but I know it had developed into a pattern by the time I was five years old. My father had a large jar in his bedroom into which he would throw change when he got home from work or from a shopping trip. There was a boy just down the street from us selling Army surplus gas masks for a dollar each. I helped myself to the money I needed and climbed out of my parents' bedroom window to avoid detection while everyone else was busy in other parts of the house. I bought the gas mask, slipped it on, and went home where I strolled through the house. Despite my attempt at a casual attitude, my father noticed the change and inquired forthwith. He made me take the mask back to the neighbor boy and tell him I had stolen the money to buy it. In addition to a long lecture from my father, I was confined to my bedroom, which just sent me back to the little world that had become my refuge. This was one of many times I would be caught and suffer the consequences of my behavior.

In kindergarten, I remember how much I liked painting. I used big, thick brushes so my strokes of paint appeared bold and confident. It was much the same as I moved through life. My words may have appeared bold and confident, but that wasn't me. That was just the way I tried to make people think I was.

I remember a boy I had asked over after school to play. We had gotten somewhat rambunctious, and we had a little battle with some raisins my mother had given us. When my father got home and saw the mess, I can still remember how embarrassed he made me feel in front of my new friend. He asked the boy what his father would do if he had thrown raisins all over their living room. Before the boy could answer, my father said, "He would probably use the belt on you, wouldn't he?" The boy looked pretty scared and went home immediately. I was also very sure he would tell the other kids at school that I had a really mean father and they had better stay away from my house. It was hard to bring friends home because they would be intimidated by my father. This intimidation would continue until my father divorced my mother and left our home. It seemed to be part of his make-up. He was a lawyer, and it was as though he never left the court-room. Talking to him was like being on the witness stand defending yourself.

By the time I was seven years old, besides being a young thief, I had fallen in love, almost been abducted, and skipped school for two days. I fell in love with a girl in another class at my school. She didn't even know I existed—I was pretty shy. I still remember the feelings I had for her at that young age. She was my first love and I had no idea where those feelings were coming from. It was a longing I didn't understand, and there was no one I could ask about it. I wrote notes to her but never had the courage to give them to her. I had no self-confidence—I was afraid of many things, and most of these things involved people.

The close call with abduction happened when my sister

and I were walking to school one morning. A very strange man driving an old beat-up car stopped and tried to talk us into riding to school with him. Fortunately, our parents had warned us about accepting gifts or rides from strangers. In looking back at it now, especially with what is happening these days, I know it could have been a very dangerous situation.

I was weaned from joy at a very early age.

When I skipped school for two days, I was in the second grade trying to avoid punishment for acting-up in class. I was supposed to stay after school but managed to slip out past my teacher, and I even took an alternate route home just in case she tried to follow me. Even at that young age I was sneaky. The next day when I left for school, I went down the block to a little girl's house and read comics all day. I told the girl's mother there was no school that day. But when I showed up at their house the next day with the same excuse, the girl's mother grew suspicious and called my mother to check on my story. That situation created one of the larger disturbances in my young life. It took a while for everyone to forget about it. The only good thing about it was in all the confusion, the teacher forgot about my initial punishment.

It seemed people kept a closer eye on me after that incident. I was sent down to the principal's office a few weeks later for "creating a disturbance in the cloakroom." The principal asked me if I was the boy who had skipped school for two days. I told him I was. He said I had already established quite a reputation for such a young child. So much for good beginnings.

When I was seven years old, my family moved from Minneapolis to St. Cloud, Minnesota, a town of about 50,000 people. My father had an opportunity to join a law firm with a long-standing reputation, a very good opportunity for an up-and-coming lawyer. The change was not a good one for me. The kids in our new neighborhood were rougher, and swaggered and swore a lot. They used some of the language I heard my father mutter on occasions of frustration or anger, but the kids in the neighborhood didn't seem to need any excuse to let go with a string of profanity. It was their form of expression, and in time it became mine.

I felt incomplete and lonely, as though I wasn't a part of things. Deep inside I was extremely sensitive, but afraid to show that part of myself to others. The part I did show, in contrast, was flamboyant and extreme, not what I really was. I began to tell stories to make the neighbor kids think I was someone special because I came from the big city of Minneapolis, and I tried to act as if I was more experienced in life. I wasn't at home nearly as much as I had been in Minneapolis, having much more time to spend with neighborhood children, and the children I picked were not a good influence. I would take risks, swagger and swear, and try to appear tougher than I could ever hope to become. This is the time I began experimenting with cigarettes, cigars, even corn silk in a pipe. It tasted terrible, but I imagined it made me appear tough. I wanted to be special in some way. I was special all right— especially troubled. I knew I wasn't a popular kid, but I wanted to be.

Not successful at being popular, I looked for some other way of getting the attention I wanted so badly. The process was gradual, but I locked onto a path that was to become a long and lonely road. I was like a machine that wasn't working properly because of a small malfunction. That malfunction, left unchecked, was rapidly becoming more and more serious.

Home life during all this time went on, but we were not a close family. I never heard the words, "I love you." In looking back, I know they were implied, but children need more than that. At least I did. I was born shortly after the war, part of the baby boom. There were many military people back in civilian life. That military training and discipline was meant for adults, but many new fathers used it as a guideline for raising their newborn children. The effects are being felt in our society to this day. Those effects, however, were somewhat more profound on me, and my reactions to them more bizarre.

True discipline requires guidance and kindness to be effective.

Discipline in our house was swift and sure and always at the hands of my father. Men did not cry or show feelings; they were tough; my father was a former sergeant in the Army. He had trained troops for duty overseas. His method was organization and order. He made us lists of jobs to do and assigned them to us, expecting us to complete them "efficiently, thoroughly, and on time"—no excuses. He was still issuing orders to the troops, and he was always finding things for us to do. As children, my brothers and sisters learned to stay away from him because if we weren't doing something "constructive," he would find us a job. On Saturday afternoons when all the kids in the neighborhood were out playing and riding their bikes, we had jobs to do. Later in life, we (as grown children) were reluctant to visit with him because there was no such thing as just "shooting the bull"—it was: "As long as you're here, why don't you help me do this." He rarely relaxed but was always doing yard work, running errands, cleaning some area, or busy at some other thing. Two or three days a week he had meetings in the evening; so he would be gone soon after supper and usually didn't return until after our bedtime, which freed us to be children.

My father came up the hard way; his mother died when he was 8 years old, and my feelings are that his father didn't give him the kind of attention and love that he needed. My father sold newspapers on the streets of St. Paul to earn money to pay for his clothing and necessities for school. He spent the majority of his time living with relatives through grade school and high school. He then went on and, through his own efforts, attended and graduated from Denver Law School. He had a great deal of motivation to "make something" out of his life. Having lacked security and love as a child may have been one of the reasons why money and security played such a large role in his life.

Being a lawyer and an ex-military man, he would draw up contracts that we'd have to sign agreeing to complete a job or change a particular behavior, etc. By the time I was 13, I'd signed so many contracts I could have been in a corporation. If we did not fulfill our end of the agreement—do what we were told—we didn't get our allowance or we'd lose some other privilege. Another problem was that my father was never satisfied with a job we did, so we did not get the rewards he had promised us. There seemed no way to win. He was especially critical of me, the oldest boy, and he focused his anger and frustration on me more and more as I grew older. No one else got beat up, no one else got hit, no one else suffered physical abuse, as far as I know. My sister tells me my hand was held over a hot burner to discourage me from smoking. I have no memory of that incident. I believe I was a convenient and safe target because I was the oldest boy. As far as I know, he didn't hit my mother or my sisters.

He did abuse my next youngest brother on occasion. We'd be sent to the woods to cut a switch from trees that would be used on our bare behinds. I remember coming in from the woods; he made us go down to the basement, pull down our pants and our underwear, and we each got ten lashes. The punishment drew blood and the welts on my butt and legs swelled up a quarter of an inch. I can't remember what we did to get that degree of punishment.

> I was tipped over and spilled as a child.

At times I would try to shift blame onto my brother if I thought I could create some doubt in my father's mind. There were times that my brother was punished when he was not even involved. This was obviously unfortunate for him. My father would say something like, "Until I find out who did it, no one is going anywhere." I'd say something like, "Okay, I'll say I did it, but I didn't." That way the family could go about their activities, and I still wasn't accepting total responsibility.

My father got me involved in a program called "Indian Guides." This was a younger version of Boy Scouts. I lost my enthusiasm for participating very quickly. I did not feel like "one of the guys." I had a feeling of being left out. I did not know what was acceptable behavior. I wanted friendships, but I did not know how to go about forming them with others. If my behavior got a reaction from someone, then I repeated that behavior because of my need for attention. It did not matter if it was acceptable behavior, I just wanted to be noticed. So my needs were met through acting out. The attention I was getting was feeding the flames of a fire of confusion that was within myself. I only remember going to a couple of meetings of the Indian Guides. My father and I just quit going. This inconsistency only demonstrates the confusion that filled my life at that time.

> A child without love is like a flower without petals.

I noticed during puberty my nipples developed lumps and I didn't know if this condition was natural. But I had heard of cancer and when I saw my father, I told him about my concern. He just chuckled and said, "Well, maybe you're turning into a girl," laughed and walked away. I didn't think of my mother as having answers to questions like that, and I was embarrassed to approach her because I had just reached adolescence and I felt kind of ignorant about it. My father could not understand or sense my need for serious consideration of my problems. I couldn't count on him to supply the answers; so I had to deal with the anxiety of wondering if I had something seriously wrong with me. A child reaching adolescence has many changes and problems to deal with. I needed reassurance; I needed to know everything was all right, and I needed to know someone cared enough to take the time to help me understand some things I was having trouble with. I needed to know I was loved. I needed that badly.

My father allowed us no weaknesses and very little expression of feelings. The quality of gentleness, so important in the positive growth of children, was absent from our lives except for brief moments spent with our mother. My father was a workaholic and did not understand our emotional needs; so it became necessary for our mother to try to provide all of these. It was a difficult and challenging responsibility with six children in our family. At times she was forced to neglect us emotionally because it was just too overwhelming for her to handle everything by herself. My father expected my mother to handle our discipline while he was at work. He expected her to clean house, prepare meals, and do the laundry for eight people; he had high expectations of everyone.

I do not look at my father as being cruel, nor do I feel he intended to do us any wrong; he was set in his way of thinking and that was that—no discussion necessary. He was only one of tens of thousands of people who were misguided about their priorities. The almighty dollar spoke very loudly in the 1950s. Although my father was a very successful lawyer, our family was a "family" only in name, not in disposition. Sharing, loving, and communicating were not evident in our home. Each of us was isolated in our own world. It was hard to get the family together without a fight. We had family meetings with contracts, rules, and job assignments but no shared moments and no teamwork.

Because our family was not close, we did not share a great deal. We, for the most part, kept to ourselves and the particular activity we might be focused on at that time. My two older sisters shared a bedroom with one another, and my younger brother and I shared a bedroom. Also, my other two youngest brothers shared a room. I never sensed any real close bonds between us kids. We put up with each other and at times shared some good moments. Whenever my brother or myself would wake up from a nightmare that had really frightened us, we would wake the other, and we wouldn't get out of bed until we had touched hands and knew we were together; then we would work our way through the darkness to the light switch, where at last we were safe. As soon as the light flooded our room, we'd breathe a sigh of relief; and the fear would dissolve in the light.

> I had high hopes when I entered this world, until I viewed the fabric, ripped to shreds and sheltered by lies.

I noticed that other families got along better, with less conflict, less yelling, fewer demands. Conflict was constant at our house, between my parents, between us kids, especially between anyone and my father. After all of us were sent to bed I would often sneak downstairs where I could get a peek at the TV. If I was quiet enough, I wouldn't be discovered. It was during some of these times that I heard my father belittling my mother for not making sure we completed an assigned job, not keeping the house clean enough, or just not doing enough to help the situation; and it seemed to me to be more of an emotional attack rather than a constructive way of solving their problems. He seemed to take out his frustration and anger on whoever was available. He had no idea what went on in that house in his absence; my mother was busy from sunup to sundown. And I am sure that some of those conversations between my father and my mother were an attempt by my mother to get our father to ease up a little on us kids, to find a different way of disciplining us. If there is one thing I learned early about my father, it's that he had great difficulty accepting criticism. He was very likely to reverse the situation and attempt to make you feel like a fool for questioning his judgment. He was an attorney, and believe me, when he questioned you or attacked your position on a particular thing, you felt just like you were on the witness stand and being questioned by the prosecution. He could destroy the composure of adults. You can imagine how effectively he intimidated us as children or a meek and gentle woman like my mother.

Things went smoothly only if we were careful not to irritate him. Each of us, in our own way, learned to live in self-imposed isolation for fear of a problem with him. I bounced against the wall early in life and later found other ways of acting out what I now know was fear—fear of being yelled at, of being sent to my room; fear of being intimidated; fear of being the target or focus of my father's anger; fear of losing privileges; fear of being slapped across the face or cornered and bullied; and also the fear of not being loved. I steered clear of my father at every opportunity; just entering a room and saying the wrong thing could set him off. He would be moody and irritable and unpredictable at times. I just never knew if it was safe to approach him or be around him, and rather than take that chance, I avoided contact with him as did the rest of the family. It isn't that we didn't love him; we just couldn't get close to him. In looking at it now, I recognize the walls around him as the same walls I built around myself as I grew and feared so much.

2 Misplaced creative energies play in hell.

NE OF MY FIRST ADVENTURES IN our new neighborhood was to set fire to a dump a short distance from our home. It was where people would haul their old papers and cardboard boxes, leaves, grass clippings, and old lumber. The dump went up like a torch. It took the boredom away for a little while as the crowds of people gathered to watch. I was enjoying the fire when an old woman emerged from the back porch of a house nearby, shouting at me and telling me she saw me light the fire; and she was going to tell the fire department when they arrived. As the sounds of the sirens screamed through the evening air, I ran away and had to watch the fire from a distance. I stayed away from that old woman's house for a long time after that and expected a fireman at our door any time. The fire had grown pretty big—bigger than I had expected. But the woman must not have known where I lived, because no one ever came for me. The neighbor kids, however, knew I had started the fire; and so my sordid reputation grew.

By the age of seven my religious training had been limited to attending Catholic church on Sundays with my mother and my sisters and brothers. My father went to a Presbyterian church across town. We generally said grace before meals if someone remembered; but our mealtimes were chaotic and did not reflect spirituality. My father was always yelling at someone. All his frustrations of the day would come home with him, and mealtime was the time he released them.

One of us might be the object of a lecture that would

escalate into an argument. Or if he heard us say something that he
didn't like, he'd be right on us. He would suddenly look up in the
middle of the meal, look around at everyone, sit up very straight
and then tell everyone to sit up straight. I got used to that look
because I always had my eye on him out of apprehension, and
when he would suddenly straighten up during a meal, I sat up as
erect as a flagpole. There were times I saw him look at me, move to
sit up straight, and by that time I had already corrected my pos-
ture. I sensed it irritated him that I anticipated his criticism. He
may not like the dress one of my sisters was wearing, or tell them
they had too much make-up on. He would ask us what we did
that day. After we told him, he would find something to criticize;
it was as though he was searching for an excuse to start trouble. It
got to a point where everyone would feel anxious until we found
out who the target was going to be that night. It came as no surprise no one wanted to share anything with him; he would pick
and pick until he drove a person nuts. There were many occasions
of people jumping up in the middle of a meal and running to their
bedroom in tears. And many appetites destroyed for food as well as
for communication with him.

I remember sitting down to eat. When the yelling would
start, my stomach would go into knots and I would lose all desire
for food, feeling physically sick. It didn't matter if I or someone
else was the focus of my father's wrath; I always felt sick afterward.
I don't have a memory of a pleasant meal. I'm sure there were
some, but what stands out in my memory was the incredible dis-
comfort. Saying grace before the meal did not improve the situation. It seemed like a farce. The contradictions were obvious.

Spirituality was a great distance away from our home. I
remember not being able to understand the concept of God and
spending a good deal of time wondering why I was here on earth
in this particular body. I began learning about death when our
family lost a bird when it drowned in a goldfish bowl after someone left its cage door open. We also lost a beautiful little puppy
when someone allowed him outside on the street without supervision. He was hit by a car and killed. These deaths gave me a sense

of how unwise it might be to have a human being managing your life, because human error had obviously caused the death of those two animals. It didn't matter who specifically was at fault; what mattered were the consequences. I did not want pets if the end result was sad and hurtful. I believed death was permanent separation and I could not fathom it being otherwise.

At this time I realized my parents were going to die. I remember how it struck me with such great force on a particular night, and I spent a long time crying into my pillow so no one could hear me. I didn't want my parents to die. The thought of it scared me tremendously, but I didn't feel comfortable trying to talk to anyone about it. What do you do with thoughts like that if you are a child and you don't have a safe place to go? I began to isolate myself even more, almost as if I were in hiding.

> I got lost in a place called loneliness;
> it was next door to despair.

I had begun to see the contradictions within myself and others. People said one thing and did another; it was a world full of inconsistencies. I remember when I heard it was wrong to be "deceptive," I didn't understand the word, but I understood the behavior, being surrounded by it. For instance, we heard a lot about patience, kindness, love, and gentleness, but people's priorities obviously were money, power and control. How valid was anything that was being told to me? Children are amazingly aware of their surroundings; they are saturated with the behavior in their environment. I found myself at this early age (seven years old), though not being aware of it, making choices based on the behavior of those around me; in other words, I was exactly as "sincere" or "insincere" as those around me. Being flexible, I was as unsound as they were. It was one of the few things I felt I had in common with others.

I was expelled from my catechism class when I was eight years old. I had lied and been discovered. Besides, I was a constant

> If we have nothing to believe in, our lives remain very empty.

behavior problem, bored to death in those classes. I could not even grasp the concept of God and here I was supposed to dedicate my life to Him. There was a great deal I didn't understand. I needed a mentor badly but didn't have one. My father began taking me to the Presbyterian church. When he gave me money for the collection plate, I pocketed it; and when I was supposed to attend Sunday school classes, I walked down a couple of blocks to an ice cream store. I never got caught, thus becoming better and better at the art of deception.

I began the fourth grade at an elementary school near our home. Things started out quietly enough, but I found myself feeling bored again and started acting up in class to get something going. Frequently I was punished for creating what the teacher called my "little disturbances." One day I must have done something especially irritating because I was told I had to stay inside during recess. It was the first time I was punished so severely. I didn't feel my behavior was so much different from that of my classmates; I was just trying to "liven things up a little!"

I spent my time during recess going through every desk in the room, just snooping. Then I decided to go through my teacher's desk. I found her purse in the bottom drawer and dug around for her billfold. Finding five dollars, I put it in my pocket. Five dollars was a lot of money to a young child in those days. I still remember how different the five-dollar bill looked with the picture of Abraham Lincoln on it. My teacher discovered the money missing before school was over for the day and asked me if I took her money. I told her I hadn't done it and headed home, sensing trouble.

My senses served me well. The teacher had called my

mother and explained what had happened. When my father got home, the interrogation began and went on for some time; but I stayed with my story. I was eventually caught spending money I was not supposed to have and, when confronted, continued to deny any guilt. I simply grew more resilient. I knew I was suspected of the theft; but I also knew that unless I admitted it, no one could be completely sure because there was no proof. It was cunning and deceptive behavior for a nine year old boy. A lot of anger was directed at me during that period. They even told me that the money I stole was for medicine for my teacher's ailing father. I remember feeling guilty, but not very guilty. My teacher told me she was going to call the police and have them investigate the theft. I didn't care, the money was gone and no one saw me take it. I stayed with my story; who could prove I was lying? I was beginning to build walls around myself allowing only a few people into my life, and the number I allowed in would gradually decrease as my life progressed.

My next serious "adventure" prompted my arrest at the young age of nine. A boy from the neighborhood came over to our house and asked if I wanted to go and have some fun. I was all for that. We headed out to explore an old, deserted building. Then we decided to see who could break the most windows by throwing rocks at them. A lot of windows shattered before the police showed up. It was my first trip to police headquarters and my friend's as well. He was a year or two older, but he was crying. The policeman poked fun at him saying "Why don't you act like your friend here and take it like a man?" I was proud of the compliment. He reinforced the lessons from my father—not to be weak or sensitive or a sissy. We got a stern lecture from the police, who then took us home and told our parents what we had done. I heard about that incident for quite a while afterwards. Whenever something went wrong in our household, I was the one under suspicion. I was beginning to get the attention I wanted.

I had two older sisters and three younger brothers. My sisters were not behavior problems—quite the opposite. They were high achievers. But my brothers and I kept the house hopping, not needing any help from our sisters. How my mother handled all the problems confronting her, I will never know. It was becoming easier to do the things I wanted without interference. I could disappear for awhile and not be missed. I was always involved in something I shouldn't be doing and utilizing my creativity in devious ways.

I started another fire in a small woods a mile or so from home. This was the largest of the several fires I set in my childhood (the first one had given me a taste for stirring up more exciting activity). There were four or five fire trucks fighting the blaze, which took about an hour to get under control. By that time the woods were half gone. It had gotten out of hand, not unlike myself. The fires created action and excitement. They interrupted the boredom I felt, but my activity was becoming more destructive.

> I was on the back road to hell.

By the time I was in the fifth grade, I was stealing jewelry from my sisters and giving it as gifts to girls I liked at school. My sisters noticed things missing from time to time but I would just deny everything. It was obvious to my family that I was the thief. My guilt was confirmed on at least two occasions when the mothers of two of the girls who had received my gifts called my mother wanting to know what a 10 year old boy was doing giving gifts of jewelry to their daughters. It was becoming embarrassing to my family to have me around. My father was fast becoming successful in his legal work, and here was his son, the thief. My behavior discredited my father's reputation. Parents who were concerned enough about my behavior to call my parents would probably be affected enough to tell their friends and neighbors about my bizarre behavior as well.

I was allowed to go to a school basketball game one fall evening. When I had to use the bathroom, it seemed only natural to also go through the belongings of the visiting basketball team. I stole a watch and a small amount of money, then I went back to watch the rest of the game. The next day as I was getting ready for school, I made the bold mistake of putting on the watch. My mother noticed it on my wrist and asked where I got the watch. I ran up to my bedroom and threw it behind a bookcase in my room, but she found it. When my father came home that night, I confessed to having taken the watch—one of the few times I confessed to anything.

> Evil is like snacks between meals: it ruins our appetite for good things.

The watch had broken when I threw it behind the bookcase, so my father had to buy a new one for the boy, which I had to deliver to the principal's office along with a very insincere apology. My only regret was that I got caught.

There were times when my father tried to be a good father. I remember once when he took my younger brother and me on a fishing trip into Canada, when we were around nine and 11 years old. One day my father and my brother were going out fishing in a fiberglass boat. I told my father I didn't want to go. I said I would just hang around our cabin while they were out fishing. After they had left, the first thing I did was find the keys for my father's car. I beat around in that for about a half an hour on the gravel roads surrounding the resort. After I had put it back, I found a .38-caliber pistol in the glove compartment of the car. I decided to do a little target practice by throwing a piece of wood off the end of one of the docks. I started shooting at it with the pistol. Needless to say, the rest of the guests that had been in the vicinity fled for shelter. They thought I was some kind of nut. After I was done shooting, I decided to look for something else to do. I wandered up to the resort office where there was a little store where people could get groceries, but nobody was around. I started digging around behind the counter and finally located the money tray in one of the drawers. I snatched up a handful of twenty-dollar bills and left very quietly. I hid the money very well just in case someone might suspect me. My father and brother didn't come back until after suppertime. I was worried because I had expected them back about four o'clock that afternoon. I was standing on the shore when I saw their boat coming toward me, but there was only one person in the boat. But, as they got closer I could see my brother's head sticking up in the front of the boat. He was sitting on the floor of the boat. I thought it was a little odd until they pulled up on the shore, and I could see my brother had sat down and stuck his buttocks into a gaping hole in the bottom of the boat. Apparently, they had hit a rock while moving along at a pretty good clip, and the only way to keep from sinking was to have my brother sit in the hole as my father operated the boat at top speed to prevent water from flowing into the hole. I thought it was funny, but my brother complained of a sore butt. My laughter subsided when my father found out I had been driving his car around in his absence. He was told about the shooting I had been doing about a hundred feet from the swimming area at the resort. I caught hell that night, but I considered it a real good day. I had quite a tidy sum of money hidden away. I had been very busy that day.

When we got back to St. Cloud after our fishing trip, I told my brother I had some money and asked him if he wanted to go ride go-carts for a while. He naturally said he wanted to go along. When we got to the go-cart track, I gave the man $50 and told him I wanted fifty tickets. They were a dollar each for about a five minute ride. No one else was there except my brother and myself, so the guy running the place just let us ride and ride. But after riding for about half an hour, I saw my father out of the corner of my eye. He had taken a load of old junk to the dump; and on his way back, he decided to stop and watch the go-carts race. A one in a million chance against that happening were about the correct odds. He thought we had spent all our money on go-carts, so he didn't search my pockets. After we got home, I got slapped around awhile, being yelled at the entire time. In looking back I think I felt I deserved the punishment I received; I did not feel like a very good person, someone who held value. I found some comfort in knowing I still had a bunch of money left. I told my father I had taken the money for the go-cart rides from his billfold earlier in the day. I didn't want him suspecting that I had robbed the resort. I seldom uttered the truth anymore about anything he asked me. I did not trust my father—not with my feelings and not with my heart. It didn't seem to matter. I usually was the target of his wrath no matter what I said, but my behavior was the fuel for that fire.

When I was 11 years old, we moved to a large house at the edge of town. It was surrounded by rolling hills and woods on three sides and a lone road that led to town. I loved the freedom when I was out exploring all by myself. I grew to know the woods very well. It felt safe and if I did not want to be found, I just went exploring. As time went by, I hid clothing, food, and a sleeping bag in places that were not noticeable by others. I knew a lot of good hiding spots. It was a big woods. Then if I needed these things, they were always there, safe and dry. I never knew when I would have more problems with my father. I had learned to "be prepared" in the Cub Scouts, an activity I had participated in briefly. It had taken on a deeper meaning in my life. I lived by my wits, so obviously those words, "be prepared," meant much more to me. I would disappear for days at a time hoping to avoid my father and his anger. I have to admit now, his anger was often justified.

It is impossible to have truth within the absence of trust.

In our new house next to the woods, my brother and I shared a bedroom on the second floor facing towards the forest. There were crows that would gather at the tops of the tall trees in the early morning and again at dusk. When my father wasn't home and my mother was downstairs cooking a meal or doing one of the many things she had to do to maintain the house, I would go into my parents' bedroom and get my father's rifle out of his closet. I would sneak it into my bedroom and remove the screen from one of my windows, load the rifle, and shoot at the crows sitting in the tops of the trees at the edge of the woods. I can remember when I

did this the first time. Afterwards, I went down to the kitchen
expecting my mother to ask what the noise was, but I guess the
rest of the household noise drowned out the sound of the gun-
shots. It was lucky I didn't kill someone. There were hills behind
the trees and someone could have very easily been walking in that
part of the woods.

I did many things that other boys my age would never
have dreamed of doing. It was about this time I began experimenting with gasoline and fire. I poured about a half gallon of gas in a
pail and set it on fire to watch what happened. I barely escaped the
flames as the gas was ignited by the match I threw into the pail.
Then in an attempt to extinguish the fire, I sprayed it with the
hose, which made the flames jump even higher.

I used to line up bullets on the sidewalk facing away from
our home toward the woods; then I would slam a hammer down
on the end of the bullet causing it to "fire," not exactly normal
stuff that you might expect from a ten or 11 year old boy.

My father had given me a bow-and-arrow set for my birthday (not a very wise decision considering the depth of my problems). I ended up shooting my brother in the foot with an arrow;
he was teasing me and saying that I wouldn't dare shoot him. He
never questioned my intent after that.

Sometimes I'd get up real early while the rest of the family
was still sleeping and head out to the woods to be there as it got
light out. I recall one such occasion. It was the dead of winter. A
beautiful winter snow had fallen overnight covering the trees and
hanging down to touch the drifts of white covering the forest floor.
Big flakes of snow slowly floated to the ground, and the air was still
and fresh. I loved the smells of the morning in the winter. I had left
home as the darkness began to fade. I carried, in a pack on my
back, a frying pan, bacon, and some eggs that I had taken from
home. I had fun gliding through the soft snow on a pair of
wooden skies, the old kind you would have to strap on. I found a
spot for a little campfire near a stump that served as my chair. After
I got the fire going and the bacon cooking, I looked up and saw a
lone pheasant sitting on a snowy branch of a tree just a few hun-

dred feet away. I remember his colors, so bright against the white backdrop. I wondered what he was doing out here all alone at this time of the morning. Then I realized he was probably wondering the same thing about me. I found peace in that woods; it was truly my refuge from the world. He probably felt the same way. I cooked my bacon and eggs and after eating, I just laid back against a tree and smoked a cigarette while the smoke from my campfire drifted slowly skyward. I watched and wondered why the world couldn't be this simple and peaceful all the time. I craved that peace and stillness. I felt safe, happy, and secure in this setting. I will never forget that morning, and I'll never forget the trouble I was in when I got back home because I had eaten an entire pound of bacon that had been meant for breakfast for the family that morning.

I started smoking cigarettes by the time I was eleven, finding it easy to conceal my behavior in the woods. But when my father smelled smoke on me, all hell broke loose. My punishment began with just a few slaps and a warning, but escalated. I was force-fed a glass of water into which my father crumpled a pack of cigarettes. This punishment happened many times. Sometimes he shoved a handful of cigarettes into my mouth and forced me to chew them up, or he washed my mouth with soap until I had huge pieces of soap stuck in my teeth. I was also beaten with branches and belts, as well as slapped around a great deal. At some point it must have become obvious to him that I would continue smoking regardless of his efforts. But the hell continued.

One night when he'd been trying to shove cigarettes in my mouth, I went to the bathroom to clean myself up. When I came back to the kitchen table, he started lecturing me again; and during the lecture he talked about his father, and I suddenly realized it was his dad that had been grampa. I had gone to his funeral and hadn't known that. I was young and did not make the connection. I remember crying uncontrollably at that realization because I was so scared about my parents dying someday. He had gone through what terrified me. "What are you crying about?" he asked. "Act like a man." I couldn't tell him. I suddenly felt ashamed for not understanding the hurt he must have felt in his loss.

Because of our move to the edge of town, I had to attend a new school. I began sixth grade. My teacher seemed an exact replica of my father, a big ex-military disciplinarian. I knew from the start that he and I were going to have problems. He must have sensed it too, because we didn't even get off on the right foot. I got the impression he didn't like me, and the feeling was certainly mutual. I tried out for the football team and made it for center position because I was tall for my age. But my teacher was the coach of the team and things were not starting out well. When one of my classmates—who lived in our neighborhood—told him I smoked cigarettes, he threw me off the team. Today we know that's the last thing we should do with a kid with problems. He should have talked to me and encouraged me to grow rather than pulling me out of an athletic activity that could have been a positive influence. I needed help and I got rejection. I was a boy with a lot of energy and enthusiasm if I felt successful at a particular thing. It would have at least been wise to attempt to channel that energy and enthusiasm in the right direction. I was getting more of exactly what I felt I was getting from my father—rejection. At the time I thought I didn't care, or at least I wasn't going to let anyone see that I did. I went back to my refuge, the woods, and lit up.

I developed a pattern of stealing money from my father's billfold in the morning while he was in the shower. I would use the money to buy gifts for girls I liked or just to act like a hotshot. Having little confidence and low self-esteem, I tried to make up for my inadequacies but only made myself look like a fool. People thought of me as different, a little weird. I guess I thought that was all right at the time. I didn't want to be average, but there was little danger of that. I continued to steal money, trying to impress others by buying them gifts. It didn't do any good, though, because I had no friends. By now I was an outsider and I knew it.

Somehow I managed to make it through sixth grade in spite of having done very little work. My teacher was pretty fed-up with me by the end of the school year. I wouldn't be surprised to learn he passed me on to the seventh grade to get rid of me. I had become a thorn in his side. Whenever he left the classroom, I would try to stir things up in any way that I could. I'd throw spit-balls, paper airplanes, or maybe a book at someone. I would get up and wander around the room, and very often I was caught by my teacher. I never did my home-work. I spent my time day-dreaming in class, wishing for what could have been instead of studying or paying attention to my teacher who would be involved in a lesson. He was constantly yelling at me to pay attention and "stop gold-bricking." I was there because I had to be, not for any other reason. And like they say, "You can lead a horse to water, but you can't make him drink." But I was learning, it just wasn't generally something my teachers shared in a lesson. It was more often about injustice, isolation, loneliness, and despair.

> Children tend to follow the paths of those who went before them.

During the summer between my sixth and seventh grade, the physical abuse from my father escalated. I understand why he became so frustrated with me. I was consistently and totally unreliable, irresponsible, and untrustworthy. In effect, I was scared and in hiding, coming out only when necessary to deal with what I had to deal with and then I would go right back into hiding. Alienated from others, I would at times lash out like a cornered animal. My behavior was a way to protect myself from my father, but he did not know that. I do not believe he intended to hurt me; he simply didn't know what to do to reach me. He was struggling to set up communication after the lines were down. I never sensed the love that is necessary in the development of a child—not from the principal, the teacher, the sheriff, the minister, the psychologist—all the people my father approached seeking help with my problems. I'd walk out of their offices and they'd be shaking their heads. As I got older, he even had some of his business associates

> When we are lost, we do not cross the paths of others, so we cannot come to know them.

talk to me. He tried to help, but the damage had already been done by then. I was very lost. I was a problem that people were trying to solve, not a human being anymore. That's how I felt. In my confusion, I was not conscious of my real needs, either.

My routine of punishment was well established. My father would send everyone to their bedrooms on the second floor of the house, including my mother. (There was no way she would have interfered. In the 1950s it was believed the man was always right. He ran the house, was the provider, and king of his castle.) He and I would go into the kitchen on the first floor and he would close the sliding door behind us. It started with talking, then yelling, then slapping me around the kitchen as I tried to cover my face with my hands. He would always yell for me to lower my hands; and when I did, he could get a clear shot at me. Eventually I stopped lowering my hands. The last thing I wanted was to cooperate with him. This was at least a weekly occurrence, and it seemed he used more force as time went on. He never hit me with his fists, although I know he was tempted. I could sense his anger and frustration. The conflict would end with him having been drained of his anger or by my mad-dash for the door to freedom and safety. I ran into the woods a lot. I was young, I was fast, and he could not catch me.

This was not the kind of childhood we dream about, but I was hardly the kind of child you would dream of having. It was as though someone left evil on the doorstep; it got into the house, then it got into me. I was every parent's nightmare and there was no waking up.

3 Our attitude is the barometer of our spirit.

 TURNED TWELVE AND STARTED SEV-
enth grade. I had heard rumors about initiations
for new students, so I prepared myself ahead of
time. I knew someone who was very large and
attended the same school I was starting, and I
paid him five dollars to watch my back. He
went with me to classes and was there at lunch
time and after school. I didn't have any problems, but I remained
alert. I was quickly learning to adapt to new situations, my flexibility grew. I began hanging-out after school with known tough
guys who had bad reputations. They were more feared than liked,
but at least they got attention, and some attention was better than
none. They became my buddies. We formed a bond of arrogance.
We hung out after school trying to look tough, smoking cigarettes
and making suggestive comments to cute girls who would pass by.
Then we'd head downtown and gather at a little Chinese restau-
rant called the OK Cafe on the main street of St. Cloud. There
were usually a group of eight or ten of us hanging around. We
would order a bunch of Cokes. We'd sit in the booths and make
our Cokes last for an hour or so and just shoot the bull and
smoke our "butts." We didn't care about anything but having a
good time. For the most part, we were from broken homes or
homes that were on the verge of breaking-up. We had no place to
go, or didn't feel that we did. It was lucky the owner of the restau-
rant put up with our noise and mess in exchange for about a dollar's worth of Cokes.

Shortly after school began, I robbed the library, taking
four or five dollars in change from the drawer where they put the

> Our sense of direction is often determined by those around us.

money for overdue books. I just waited until no one was looking and opened the drawer, took the money and left. The librarian came to the room where I had my next class and pulled the teacher aside. With a glance at me, he called my name and I knew I was in trouble. I still had the money in my pocket and when I tried to tell the teacher it was mine, he wouldn't believe me. Who carries four to five dollars in pennies, nickels, and dimes in their pockets? I was taken the principal's office where they made a call to my mother. I was suspended for three days. Naturally, my father and I had one of our sessions. After things had cooled down, I realized I had three days off from school—a pretty good deal. But my father made a large list of jobs to keep me busy.

Eventually I was back in school, but I had established a reputation. The whole school seemed to know what I had done. I tried to act like I didn't care, but I did. My self-esteem went down another notch. The walls around me were becoming bigger and stronger to keep the pain out, but they kept the pain in and the people out.

About this time my father began to go away on business trips more often. I looked forward to his leaving because of the relative peace it would bring to our house. When he was gone, I was pretty much free to do what I wanted. Although my mother didn't approve of some of my activities, there wasn't much she could do to stop me. She had five other children to raise and a very large house to maintain. Her hands were full. I was reasonably respectful of my mother most of the time, but with behavior problems like mine coupled with my attitude and size, it was not smooth sailing for her. She often tried to get through to me, but I just wouldn't listen. At that point in my life I thought I had all the answers. It would be a long time before I learned what a serious mistake that was.

My mother demonstrated some of the better qualities to be found in people. She was kind and caring and very unselfish; she would never take the last serving of food, for instance, even if she was still hungry—the children always came first. She also accepted the notion that the husband was in charge. So much so that, had we had a different father, my mother would have probably spoiled us. My father's authority was not questioned; and if it was, there were guaranteed repercussions. Compared to the power and intimidation my father wielded, my mother's qualities appeared weak and fragile. It was clear to me the controlling power seemed to be in the hands of those who were the most ruthless and had only their own best interests at heart and the strength to back their actions up, much like the world in general.

I liked the nights I spent by myself in the woods. I would spend hours just watching the stars at night, amazed at the immensity of it all. I'd hear the animals as they went about their nighttime activities. They never seemed to be flustered by my presence; they grew used to me. There were chipmunks and squirrels that would come right up to get a morsel of food from my hand. Sometimes I would watch storms roll in, and I'd watch how the lightning illuminated the forest with its brightness. I loved high winds; the power and force that broke branches and uprooted old trees was a source of excitement for me. The thunderstorms and winds seemed to fill me with new life. I felt as though I was given strength by the power in the air. I felt like the woods was my home; I felt safe there

and peaceful inside, at least a lot more peaceful than I did at home with my father around.

But when I was away from home I didn't have enough money for food or cigarettes, and I had to steal. I would go through the garages and cars in the neighborhood, taking anything of value I could find. I was very proud of my ability to move around at night without detection. Living in my own private little world, I often likened myself to Tom Sawyer. The only thing missing was "ole Huck Finn" and the raft on the river.

One thing I liked to do was read. It was a primary source of pleasure, filling something deep inside me and giving me an escape from painful reality. In the third grade when we were supposed to do a total of four book reports for the year, I had turned in more than thirty. By the time I had finished sixth grade, I'm sure I had read at least a hundred books. They were a refuge.

I began burglarizing homes in the neighborhood, a small step from cars and garages. I would usually find a door or window unlocked; I was very determined. As my life moved forward, I would come to learn many ways of breaking into a home or business, how to hot-wire a car, or how to shoplift to get the money I would need for some of the "habits" I would come to be involved in. I would usually take money, jewelry, and the liquor; I had no use for anything else. Although I didn't drink then, I knew older boys who did and they were willing customers. I remember that I hurriedly stashed jewelry under rocks, in a tree limb or in a hole somewhere, a place that might become hard to locate after a while. Some of it I never found when I went back for it. Some of these things were treasured keepsakes in people's lives; I didn't care. When I had enough money, I would stay at the Germain Hotel which was right in the middle of downtown St. Cloud, Sometimes I would stay at small motels

> When we anticipate conflict, we have already made a decision.

just at the edge of town to avoid detection from people who might know me. If a desk clerk asked questions because I appeared very young, I would just tell him my parents were on vacation and I had just returned from summer camp and needed a place to stay until they returned. I never had any problems. I would just lie around smoking cigarettes, watching television, and ordering food from room service if I was at the hotel; or I'd call and order a pizza.

> If ignorance were bliss, we would see a great many more smiles on the faces of those we meet in this world.

Slowly I was learning the art of manipulating others to get what I wanted. It had become second nature for me to lie; but sometimes I was amazed that people believed me because my stories were so far from the truth. There were times when I was carrying a lot of cash around for a 12-year-old boy, and you would have thought someone might have suspected something by the way I spent money on room service or at restaurants. I also rode around in a cab if I wanted to go somewhere. After three or four days of this extravagance, people would generally start wondering a little about my lifestyle. But if I sensed someone was suspicious, I would just move to another hotel or motel.

All I cared about was getting by—no matter who was affected or what were the consequences. Cold and callous out of necessity, I felt totally alone and sure that no one cared about me. I also felt I was not deserving of anyone's care and concern. Who could blame people for disliking me; I knew I held little value.

I turned thirteen and my behavior became more engrained, more clearly defined, with a firmer direction. I became boisterous, aggressive, and arrogant. Once, I got in a fight because

I didn't like the way someone looked at me. I only had to hit him once; I don't think he ever looked at me again. He didn't want to fight; and when I sensed his fear, I felt more confident and lashed out at him. I had such a low self-image, I thought people were talking about me and making jokes about me. I was always on the offensive—attacking before I could be attacked. People would go around me rather than pass by me. I mistook fear for respect and, in my arrogance, thought I had all the right answers.

> Ignorance is only vast when it is given room to grow.

On one of my frequent absences from home, I met two old men who owned a farm a short distance beyond the woods surrounding our neighborhood. They raised and sold vegetables from their farm. It was a place to hang out, and they paid me thirty-five cents an hour to work for them. I would pick and sell vegetables to their customers, generally pocketing enough money to help me survive. They were both in their sixties and single with a big, old house; so they would let me stay there when I needed a place to stay. They spent a lot of time alone. They were both a little odd and very quiet. For a while I hung around with one of them. We would go to the movies or wander around downtown, but neither of us had extra money to do anything special. We just wandered around aimlessly. Then the old fellow bought a cheap car and if we could afford the gas, we went riding around. This routine continued through the summer and into the school year.

One day I wouldn't get out of the driver's seat of his car. I told him I was going to drive today. He didn't like it at all, but he had no choice if he wanted to go anywhere because I wasn't moving. So he taught me how to drive. I felt like quite a hotshot driving around in a car when I was only 13 years old. Luckily, we weren't caught. He didn't have a license, either.

After that, I began to take my father's car out for a quick spin when he was out of town on business. My mother wasn't aware of these little trips. I would only go after dark. I would get in and put the car in neutral and push it out of the driveway. Once I got it in the street, I could safely start it up without alerting my mother. I don't think my father ever noticed because stealing his car was something even *I* wouldn't do (or so he thought). He didn't realize I had reached a point where I was taking full advantage of every situation that presented itself. If I had access to his keys or his money or anything else I felt that I needed, I took it. No guilty conscience to deal with, just the reality of my attitude and the belief that I was entitled to anything I wanted, and it didn't matter whose it was. I was pretty hard on that car, constantly "laying rubber" with it. The transmission went out shortly after my father got the car and was replaced by the dealer. I have no doubt that my abuse of the car was responsible for that particular mechanical failure.

One of the times I had been staying at the old fellows' house, my father's car pulled into their driveway. I thought he had come to try to take me home. Instead he told me that he had packed his things, and he was moving out and I could go back home now if I wanted to. His revelation came as a shock. I remember feeling relief, although it is sad to admit it. At first, I thought it might be some kind of a trick to get me back home. I told my father I would stay where I was. He said I should think about it and drove off. So, I headed home to see if he had told me the truth. When I got home, I went up to my parents' bedroom to see if my father's clothes were gone from his closet. They were. I breathed a sigh of relief, although I knew my mom was not happy. That night I stayed at home, but things were

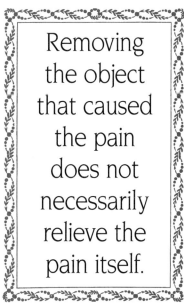

Removing the object that caused the pain does not necessarily relieve the pain itself.

different now. I was surprised to find there was an empty spot inside me with my father gone. I was not happy with him around, and I missed him when he was gone. It was confusing. My father came back a week or so later, a pattern that would repeat itself many times.

I turned 13 and began the eighth grade at South Junior High. I felt uncomfortable being around so many people. I knew some of the students from my previous school, but I wanted to be alone or around just a few people. In school I felt closed in like a caged bird. I started hanging out with a guy a year older than me who had a reputation of being tough. We'd hang out before and after school just smoking cigarettes and "shooting the bull" with the other "outsiders." We were not the type of students who went directly to their classroom when they arrived at school. We waited to enter the school until the last minute, attempting to avoid the inevitable.

About the second week of school, we decided to skip school and go downtown. On our walk into town, we decided to steal a car. I don't remember who thought of the idea, but in ten minutes we had found a car with the keys in the ignition. We just went beating around in the country. My buddy was driving too fast and we slid into a ditch. We walked over to a farmer and asked him to pull us out. We told him we would come back later that day to give him some money. Of course, we never did go back there; but the police did.

We had abandoned the car about a mile from the farmer's house and the police went from farm to farm asking if anyone knew anything. Once they had our descriptions, they checked the schools for absentees. We were arrested the next morning at school. The police separated us and used the old trick of saying that the other guy confessed so you might as well tell us the truth too. We were young and inexperienced, so it worked easily on us. After we signed our confessions, I was given a ride home by a detective who talked to my father and gave him a copy of my confession. When that detective left, all hell broke loose. He yelled about me being "bigtime" now that I had stolen a car. I can't really remember at this time if I got hit, but it seemed to go along with the territory; it was an integral part of the process that my father used as a "remedy" for my behavior. It was no wonder he was so outraged. Here was a wealthy, respectable lawyer living in a posh, new addition of town, driving a brand new car, and earning enough money to buy all the things a person could want, with a son who had been soiling the family reputation for years. Everyone in our family was embarrassed and ashamed by my behavior. My brothers and sisters would say things at the kitchen table at supper time that they had heard in school about some of my antics. All of our neighbors and my parents' friends were aware of my "unmanageability" (this was a kind word for the madness I had been swept up in.) It had been going on too long to remain a secret. My name meant trouble. I didn't blame them for their feelings. They worked hard to get the respect and the friendships they had and along came Tom to make not only himself look like a fool but everyone else in the family as well. I was, in spite of my outward appearance, very sensitive to everything, so I was hurt by their shame for me. I was just totally out of control.

I went to juvenile court about two weeks after we were caught for stealing the car. The judge put me on probation, which meant I had to report to a probation officer every week. My probation officer would ask how I was doing, and I would tell him everything was fine, even when things were not going well. The last thing I needed was to call further attention to myself. Having my father on my back all the time was enough; I didn't want any more contact with "the law" than was necessary. The judge told me if I had any further problems, he would send me to Red Wing Reform school. I had heard how tough

The reality of hell expressed itself dramatically in my life.

reform school was. I didn't want to experience it, so I tried not to make waves. But then I got caught smoking in the bathroom at school, and I was suspended from school. That incident was all the judge needed. My probation officer took me to reform school two days later, and it was just the beginning. I was 13 years old and if I had known what lay ahead in my life, I believe I would have ended it, because I was entering thirty years of hell.

4 Suffering creates compassion.

THE FIRST THING I NOTICED WHEN I arrived at reform school was that all of the doors were locked behind me. I felt like a trapped animal; I had never been anywhere I could not get out of. And there were people watching my every move. To make matters worse, the entire reform school was surrounded by high bluffs covered with rocks and trees. They had planned well when they built this place. It would have been difficult to run away. There were about nine cottages with about 35 boys in each cottage, arranged so that boys of approximately the same age would be together. I found out later that I was one of only two 13 year old boys in the entire place. The average age was about sixteen. I was tall for my age so that helped me to feel less threatened.

In each cottage the counselor selected two or three of the biggest boys to help supervise the others. These guys were called "belts," an appropriate name considering their responsibilities. If a boy tried to make a break for freedom, the belts would give chase; and when they caught him, they would work him over pretty good. It was primitive but effective. The belts would also make sure we stayed in line on the way to the dining hall or when we left the cottage for any supervised activity. They were just there to help the staff "kick ass" when necessary. Sometimes people who were already bullies got these jobs, so their negative behavior was praised and reinforced. The error was obvious as were the consequences. I saw boys smaller than myself getting kicked or beaten with fists just because they were not well-liked, and they made no effort to defend themselves. The moment bullies discover that their victim will strike back, they look for another victim. They don't want confrontation; they want control. Some of the boys suffered serious emotional damage during their stay there.

I remember well the first letter I wrote home. It was on the same evening I got there. It was my first experience of having tears fall on the pages of a letter I was writing, and it wouldn't be the last. It was probably the most difficult thing I have ever written. I begged my parents to get me out of there with every promise I could make. I hurt so bad that I could not keep the tears from falling on the letter, but the last thing I wanted was for someone to catch me crying. Weakness leaves you wide-open to potential predators, and there was no shortage of those in reform school.

We slept in a dormitory with a night watchman keeping an eye on us all night. I pulled the blankets over my head and cried myself to sleep. No longer the tough guy, I was filled with overwhelming loneliness and I missed my family terribly. Waking up there in the morning was like waking up in hell. We would get up at six o'clock in the morning and go down several flights of stairs to the locker room and shower area. There were four toilets lined up against the wall with no partitions—absolutely no privacy. When your turn came to use a toilet, the boys waiting in line would tell you to hurry up. Regular bowel movements were out of the question. I was constipated and felt ill for the first several weeks.

> When we cannot see nor sense an end to our terror, there is little hope in our hearts.

My head was shaved the first day and I was issued "state" clothes, and poked and prodded by a doctor. Feeling and looking like a prisoner of war, I was assigned to the "spud room" for the first two weeks. My job there was to peel potatoes all day long. We needed enough potatoes to feed about five hundred people twice a day. That was a lot of potatoes. It gave me time to think and to

daydream. I will never forget the smell of all
those potatoes and the looks of the boys peel-
ing them. We were all "new" boys and there
was no happiness on any of our faces.

Occasionally, they would call me from
the spud room to take some tests to determine my
needs and how they could help me meet those needs.
Although that statement sounds very helpful, what it really means
is how they, the system, could contain me and keep me occupied
during that containment to keep my mind off creating problems
and/or attempting an escape. Each new arrival got a series of sixteen shots because those in charge went on the assumption that no
one had ever had any vaccinations in their life. There were numerous tests to figure out what to do with me. I was glad for anything
that got me away from the smell of potatoes.

I longed for people I knew, especially my family. I can
remember wondering why I had to go through this punishment.
What had I done that was so wrong? I did not believe I was a bad
person or that I deserved to be there. I was hoping I would wake
to find it had been a bad dream. It was just too painful to be real. I
felt emotionally abandoned, like a dying plant craving nourishment and something to quench its thirst. I kept to myself. It was
the only place I felt safe.

After the first two weeks had dragged by, they told me I
would be continuing my schooling during half of the day, and
would be assigned to the barber shop for training as a barber for the
remainder of the day. Training a 13 year old boy for barbering
seemed stupid, but I didn't care. I figured it would give me some
variety in my day. The schooling seemed to be several levels below
where I had been, so I had no difficulty doing the work. I ended up
with a lot of free time, so I could read and daydream. The books let
me escape to other places, which probably helped me to keep my
sanity. Reform school was filled with some really strange people.
There were boys who would just mutter to themselves and most of
the time didn't make a lot of sense. There were bullies, sex perverts,
boys already so addicted to drugs that they would put anything into

their veins to get high. The list could go on and on. I remember one boy who made a syringe out of an eyedropper by filing the end of the glass tube into a point so it was sharp enough to insert into his veins. He would inject whatever he could find in the way of dope. Once, when he couldn't find anything else, he injected lighter fluid; I heard later that he had become paralyzed for life. Red Wing Reform School was where the State of Minnesota put the most incorrigible juvenile offenders, some of whom should have been confined to mental hospitals. Later on some of them *would* end up in those places after having committed some very violent offenses, such as murder and rape. As I grew older, I heard the names of boys that I had known in reform school on the news reports or read about them in the paper having been arrested for committing violent crimes. Occasionally, I would hear about one of them killed in a shootout with police or a drug rip-off.

When school was over, we went to the dining hall for lunch, which consisted chiefly of bread and potatoes. They gave us some meat, but I couldn't tell what kind of meat it was most of the time. Then we would go back to the cottage and sit around for half an hour. Boys 16 years old or older could smoke four cigarettes a day, after meals and before bed, if they had their parents' permission. The cigarettes were kept under lock and key all of the time, and used as a control device by the staff. If there were behavior problems, the boys lost their cigarette privileges. The severity of the offense would determine the duration of that loss.

Here I was locked up in reform school because I was thrown out of school for smoking; and the reform school allowed and, in effect, *encouraged* the boys to smoke! Extra cigarettes were used as rewards for good behavior—just another example of the irony of my life.

After lunch, we went to our work assignments. In my case, it was the barber shop. I learned in the beginning that we were not going to be taught the finer points of cutting hair. We were given the clipper with three plastic attachments which cut the hair to three different lengths. New boys got the shortest cuts, a shaved head. Everyone else got one of two different lengths, short or

General view of Red Wing Correctional Facility (in 1961), taken from the bluffs overlooking the Mississippi River (in background). PHOTO COURTESY OF RED WING CORRECTIONAL FACILITY

shorter. It was not the kind of job that created friendships. I would meet a boy, and the first thing I did was shave his head. But I kept my mouth shut and did my work.

The old guy that trained us was a rough character. He told us stories about some of his exploits in his younger days when he had been a pretty wild kid. I could tell that underneath all that gruffness was someone who cared for people a great deal. He would yell and cuss like a crazy man but it was just a show to keep things lively. As the weeks and months passed by, he sometimes gave a gray day a little sunshine. There were many gray days, though.

I started seeing a psychologist about once a week. All I ever did in his office was cry. It was the one spot I could be almost alone. It was always the same. I'd come into his office, start talking, and then start crying; and I didn't stop until he told me my time was up. Then I would go back to school or to the barbershop and wait until next week when it would be safe to cry again. At first I had a lot of hurt and fear in my life. Now it was turning to anger. I felt that I had never done anything to hurt anyone as badly as they were now hurting me. Those around me were trying to shape and form me. It seemed the whole idea of this place was to get a person to do as he was told without argument. They were attempting to make us submissive; it wasn't going to work on me—on the outside, maybe, but not on the inside. I resented not being born into a "normal" family. I did not feel I was a bad person; I felt that I had a difficult or even impossible situation to deal with at home. I didn't necessarily believe that I alone was the problem. I was learning about justice, man's justice; and the more I learned, the more I hurt. I knew it wouldn't do any good to tell people that the only thing I ever wanted was to be safe and loved and happy, because I didn't feel that anyone gave a damn anyway.

> Ignorance is not having a correct understanding of goodness. Stupidity is doing something we know is wrong— but we do it anyway.

Thanksgiving in 1961 goes down in my history as one of the emptier days of my life. I thought of my family and what they would be doing. I was missing the togetherness, however meager it had seemed to be in the past. It didn't appear quite so meager under these circumstances. Thanksgiving had been one of the emotionally safer and more enjoyable days we had together as a family. Everyone's mood was better in the holiday season. We were much more of a family at those times. In reform school we had turkey and dressing for lunch, and we saw a movie in the gymnasium. None of that helped make me feel less alone.

The month of December passed very slowly because I was so conscious of Christmas approaching. It should have been the best time of the whole year with everyone in a good mood, excitement in the air, Christmas carols, special movies on television, and dreaming of the gifts we would receive. I had nothing but emptiness and vast sadness because of where I was; the feelings of Thanksgiving were multiplied ten times over. I remember the night before Christmas: a group of young people from a local church came in to sing carols, and about half of them were girls. I was surprised to hear girls' voices singing! It sounded so different than just us boys singing. I'd been in that place too long. The last days before Christmas were almost as bad as Christmas itself. I was constantly thinking of what my family would be doing and how badly I wanted to be with them.

> When our lives feel empty, they generally are—not unlike a room with no furniture and no purpose.

Christmas Eve, I pulled the covers over my head and cried very quietly. One of the other boys hollered my name. I wiped away my tears and looked over at him. He was rubbing his eyes and laughing, calling me a cry baby. Other boys laughed at me too. I was struck by their cruelty. I hurt enough. I know that some of those boys laughing at me probably cried themselves to sleep that night as well. I'm sure I was not the only boy there with feelings of homesickness.

Christmas morning, I wished I'd never woken up. All I could think of was my family and how much I was missing by not being with them. I had received a package of presents from home, but it only made that feeling of loneliness and isolation stronger. I would have been affected less emotionally had I not received this package. I felt like a container filled with sorrow and pain. To make things worse, one of the bigger guys asked me if he could have some of the Christmas cookies and pop that my parents had sent to me. I told him he couldn't and he punched me in the face. It was the hardest anyone had ever hit me. I was almost knocked out. As he walked away, I felt very sorry for myself; but now I understand more. No one had sent him any gifts because his parents were divorced and his mother didn't have any money. He never got any visits, and letters from home were few and far between. But it was hard to consider another person's feelings when I felt such loneliness and fear.

I was glad when the Christmas season was over. It was a relief. I continued going to school and working at the barber shop. It was January and I would appear before the parole board in February. These people would determine if I stayed at reform school or went somewhere else. Their options were to keep me in reform school, send me to a foster home, or send me back home to live with my family. I hoped they would send me home, but my caseworker recommended that I be sent to a foster home. He viewed the situation at home as a poor environment. He had all the reports that had been done by my probation officer and the courts in my hometown of St. Cloud. He also had all the results of the tests that I had taken since my arrival. And he had spent several hours talking to me. The problems at home were very obvious, but I didn't care where I went as long as I got out of this constant confinement. I was extremely cooperative.

It was the dead of winter, so we didn't get much exercise, except when we had gym class. Then we would play basketball or participate in some other high-intensity activity. Our instructor had been in reform school when he was a boy. He was a good guy. He demanded a lot from us, but we had fun, which was rare in there. He told us once that one out of ten of us would be dead by the time we were 18 years old—those were our odds. He turned out to be right in his prediction, but, in my opinion, his estimate was a bit low. As I traveled through the "system," I would watch as one by one someone I knew was killed or died; and these were not natural deaths. These boys had overdosed on drugs, were killed while drunk and driving a stolen car, or shot during an armed robbery, burglary, or some other criminal activity. These were all very real possibilities for me. My lifestyle was very similar to their own.

February came and my excitement grew as the date of my parole hearing approached. By now I had told my caseworker I thought a foster home would be the best thing for me, too. Even though I didn't want to go anywhere but home, I figured I had better concentrate on getting out of this place, not where I went. I also felt that if the people on the parole board thought I wanted to go right back to my prior setting, they would think I wasn't ready to get out. I was being careful, learning the game, trying not to make waves. I could not risk problems: if they decided I'd have to stay in reform school, I'd automatically receive three more months.

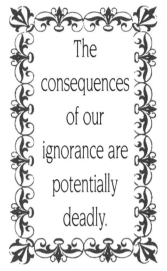

The consequences of our ignorance are potentially deadly.

I tried to look neat, clean, and polite when I finally appeared at my parole hearing. I wanted them to see a nice, young, innocent boy who belonged somewhere else, anywhere else, just not here. They approved the plan for a foster home placement just as my caseworker had recommended. I still wanted to go home, but I told them the foster home idea was the best choice. They told me that as soon as they could find a foster home to take me, I could go; but I knew of boys who had waited six months and longer to get placed in an acceptable foster home. At least I knew I was finally getting out. Still I was impatient.

About two weeks later, my probation agent came to see me. He told me my father had contacted him and my family wanted me to come home instead of going somewhere else. He said the parole board had approved the change in plans, and I could go home.

As soon as he got the paperwork done. About a week later, I got called from school to go over to my cottage. There wasn't a "belt" escorting me, which was unusual. As I suspected, this was the moment I had been waiting for. I was to get into my own clothing and be ready for the bus in an hour. I can't describe that feeling of being in my own clothes, waiting to go home. I had only been at reform school for about four months. It was February 15, 1962, but it seemed like I had been gone a lifetime. In two months

Red Wing Correctional Facility (1960s). (Top) Typical inmates' cottage; (bottom) boys' dining hall.

PHOTOS COURTESY OF RED WING CORRECTIONAL FACILITY

I would turn 14 years old.

They gave me a ride to the bus depot in Downtown Red Wing and a ticket to Minneapolis where my father, who was there on business, would pick me up at the bus depot. He would take me back home to St. Cloud. It felt so good to be free. I remember thinking that I was really going to try to make an effort to do what I was supposed to do. I never wanted to go back to reform school again. My intentions were good. I was on an emotional high.

> We can advise others on which direction to travel, but we cannot attempt to make that journey for them.

The first thing I did after I got to the bus depot was get a pack of cigarettes. I smoked most of them before I got to Minneapolis. I had really missed smoking. At 13 years old, it had really become a habit. When my father found me at the bus depot, I must have smelled like a smokestack. After he shook my hand and greeted me, he asked if I had been smoking. I said, "No." But as I spoke, I blew a small cloud of smoke right in his face. He knew I was already lying, and I hadn't even arrived back home yet.

As we drove to St. Cloud, we talked a little, but it felt like we were strangers. It was just after dark and the roads were covered with ice and snow. I was afraid we would slide off the road and be killed in an accident. In my mind, I asked him to slow down; but I knew it wouldn't do any good to say anything. My fears were more or less ignored, not dealt with.

My father told me that the eldest of the two farmers I had lived with near our home had died in an accident involving his truck. He was pulled from his truck, which had burst into flames after the accident and he would have been safe; but for some

reason he pulled away from his rescuers and ran back to the truck
and got in. He was burned to death. I wondered what had drawn
him back to the burning truck. He wasn't a happy person, but he
had been a good friend regardless of our age difference. We had
connected somehow. I would miss him.

The rest of the trip was quiet. I think we both felt uneasy.
We hadn't talked in a long time. We arrived at our house about 7
o'clock that evening. I will never forget the funny look of recognition on my youngest brother's face. He came running to the front
door as I opened it, looked at me for a few seconds, and then
shouted, "Tom!" I knew he had not recognized me at first; I had
been gone four months, and that's a long time for a little boy. But
I'll never forget his smile of recognition and the happiness I felt at
the time. It was good to be home. My family had waited until I
got home to have supper, so we sat at the table and had a pretty
quiet supper. After supper, my mom brought out some presents
that had been put away for me since Christmas. That was a nice
surprise; although, the Christmas I missed could never be
replaced.

After things had leveled off a little and people were used
to having me home, I went outside quietly to have a cigarette. My
father came out a different door of the house and discovered me. I
thought all hell would break loose again, but he just said we
should start out with a new beginning and he did not want me
smoking anymore. I was really hooked on cigarettes. I always
wished my father would not make it such a big issue; it just created more problems. I was only thirteen, but I wished everyone
would forget about my smoking and let me get on with life. The
fact that these feelings were coming from a 13 year old boy should
not have made any difference. They were my feelings, and they
had to be dealt with. I was beginning to resent the attempts of
others to control my life, and that resentment was growing fast. I
had come out of reform school a different boy than the one that
went in there. I thought I had learned a lot. I thought I had all
the answers. And not only that, but I was now a confirmed
"tough guy," or thought I was, because I had been to reform

school. My reputation was making me notorious, but at least I got the attention I wanted so badly.

> What is injected into our hearts when we are young, is later injected through the rest of our being as well: love-hurt, peace-pain, laughter-tears, courage-fear, hope-hopelessness.

I went back to school and bragged about having been to reform school. I'd been around; I knew the program. If my peers didn't like me, I at least wanted their respect, and I thought I could gain their respect by bragging about my "adventures" in reform school. Inside, however, I had a low opinion of myself. I had no friends, no girlfriends, no social exposure with females. I had moved around so much that I had had no opportunity to form lasting friendships. I was becoming desperate for human companionship and love, so I acted unacceptably to get it. I never felt confident with who I was.

I never did my homework when I was in school. I would manage to get grades that were just passing. I'm sure I was shuffled along with the others in my classes just to keep me moving. I wasn't by any means the teacher's pet. I was more of a nuisance than anything else. I was always trying to get out of work and trying to stir up some excitement. I felt that school was absolutely the most boring place I had ever experienced. Six or seven hours in a classroom each day was not my idea of fun. I felt I had better things to do.

Once I had learned to read and write, I was pretty much off on my own. I never had any problems with basic math. So as far as I was concerned, the rest of the classes were a waste of my time. The word "contempt" aptly describes how I felt about school. I somehow managed to complete my eighth year of school

and was passed on to the ninth grade. Summer quickly
approached. I had just turned 14 years old.

5 Lessons do not come with mercy; mercy comes from lessons.

HE PROBLEM WITH HAVING FREE TIME when my father was around was that it was no longer "free." He always kept us busy. He thought that activity would keep us out of trouble. He would make lists of jobs he wanted done each day before he left for work. I never understood why he could not just let us be kids and have fun. Even if the jobs were completed, they were very seldom completed to his satisfaction.

I remember one particular day when my father had left instructions for one of my brothers and me to do the yard work. We were to cut and trim the lawn. We spent almost the entire day working, hoping he would be impressed by our efforts. We did an extra-good job and did many things we were not even asked to do. We were really proud of the job we had done. But when our father got home, he immediately criticized the job. He hadn't even made it from his car in the driveway to the front door before he asked us what we had been doing all day. We were very disappointed kids.

My mother heard what was happening and came out and told my father how hard we had been working all day. Later on he praised some of the work, but the damage was done. It left me feeling like I shouldn't even bother to begin anything he asked me to do; he would never be satisfied with it anyway. It was totally frustrating for me.

Praise was hard to come by. Praise is something children thrive on. My father meant well. I really think he tried, but he just had more negative things to say than positive. I believe he was overwhelmed with the responsibility of such a large family and his work. He worked hard; it seemed like he worked all the time. Six children are emotionally demanding on their parents; it's like a small daycare center for children today. My father's commitment was to his work. He never for a moment realized the responsibility that would be coming along with a large family. He was having trouble managing both of those responsibilities in his life. I was evidence of that.

> In a person of stone, we must look deeply to see the tears, but they are there.

When the conflicts would develop between my father and me, I would solve the problem by running away to the woods. I spent a lot of time in that woods during the summer of 1962. It didn't matter if I was caught smoking, said the wrong thing, or hadn't completed one of my tasks properly. Any problem with my father would escalate out of control quickly, because of my attitude and his anger. We were a poor combination. We never communicated with one another. We were completely out of harmony, something I believe neither of us knew anything about. I had my usual "stash" in the woods—extra clothing, food, and a sleeping bag. I liked waking up early and watching the sun come up. The smell of the air was so fresh in the morning. I would have stayed right there in that woods if I hadn't needed anything else to survive. But I had to eat and I needed money to support my smoking habit; so I would go out wandering at night looking for homes that were empty where I could get the things I needed—and things I didn't necessarily need but could sell to get some cash.

I didn't have anyone I could really call a good friend, someone I knew I could count on, so I spent the majority of my time alone. I spent a lot of time daydreaming about everything imaginable. Inside of myself was a safe place where no one could get in and I could find a degree of happiness. My imagination became my only friend.

There was nothing the least bit glamorous in the way I lived. I usually didn't have enough money or food. There would be times when I was able to steal enough to keep me going for a few days. I usually spent the money foolishly on things I didn't really need. I'd stay in a hotel or motel and order food to be delivered. Then the money was gone and I was broke again. It developed into a pattern that summer. By September, I was on the run from the police for burglaries I had committed, so I hid in the woods. I had a few close calls when the police almost caught me, but I was fast. I was almost six feet tall by the time I was fourteen, and skinny as a rail. If there was anything I could do well at that age, it was to run. More than once I had heard cops cursing at me as they had to give up the chase. There was no way any of those guys could have kept up with me. They knew I hung out in the woods, but it was large and I knew every inch of it. Once when they were after me, I was hidden in some brush. I could hear them stop about ten feet from me and try to decide what to do, now that they had lost me. It was a challenge for me, and it helped to create diversity in my day.

> I hear the most inside the silence of myself. It is where I go most often; and it is a quieter, gentler place.

It started to get colder outside, so I decided to turn myself in, hoping they would give me a break. They gave me a break all right, a break in the county jail until the next day when my parole officer would return me to Red Wing Reform School. Back to hell.

Nothing had changed at reform school, except I knew my way around a little bit better than I did the first time. I knew the game. The name of the game was manipulation.

I was at reform school for about six weeks before the parole board decided to send me to a foster home. I knew they suspected problems at home that might be contributing to my difficulty, so I told them what they wanted to hear. Then the waiting for a suitable foster home began. It took about a month.

A probation officer from another part of Minnesota came to see me. They were not going to send me anywhere near my family. The agent told me I had a choice of two foster homes—one with a minister and his family, or one with a young couple who owned a farm. I chose the farm, thinking it would be the lesser of two evils. He said he would arrange for the transfer, and I should be on a bus in a week or so. This was good news: even if I wasn't going home, at least I was going to get out of this hell hole.

Arrangements were made, and I was on a bus in a week. My new parole officer picked me up, and we drove to the farm which was going to be my new home. It was in the "boonies," twenty miles to the nearest town. I felt like I was fighting a never-ending battle and wondered what had happened to my childhood.

When I arrived, they had a hired hand. But they let him go the next day. I was now their hired hand. Not only that, but the State was going to give these people money for taking care of me. So I got up at five in the morning, did chores, ate breakfast, and then took the bus to school. After school I would take the bus home, do my chores until about 7:30 in the evening, eat supper, and go to bed. On weekends, we just worked longer hours. I didn't know what was the better choice: reform school or this place. These people objected to my smoking as much as my father did, so the battle began. That farmer took enough cigarettes from me to support his own habit. I would sneak around to have a quick cigarette, and he would sneak around and catch me.

Finally, they gave in after about six months of their game of cat-and-mouse, and they agreed if I didn't get into any further trouble, I could smoke cigarettes. Shortly after that the father of the man I was staying with was driving the tractor while I was pulling and piling bales of hay onto a hay wagon in about 90 degree heat. When things slowed down for a few minutes, I lit a cigarette and started smoking it. Then this guy's father yelled at me to put the cigarette out. I still remember what he said, "When you can do a man's work, you can smoke like a man." I'd been doing a man's work daily for the past six months. This guy was sitting on the tractor on his butt; I was the one doing all the work. I was getting real sick of people and believed I had every reason to feel that way.

I had been stealing anything I could at school so I could support my smoking habit. I had also skipped school a few times and not been caught. None of the kids liked me at the school I went to. I was boisterous, obnoxious, and always looking for a fight if anyone even looked at me wrong. I did not know how I appeared to others, or I might have changed my ways a bit. I lied about things to try to impress people. I felt so inadequate, and I was continuing to try to make up for my feelings of inadequacy by pretending I was something I was not. I was struggling for acceptance, but my struggle was in vain. I didn't understand what would make me acceptable. I needed guidance badly, and I felt so isolated, a bad combination.

I was suspected of stealing from my classmates. No one had seen me, but it didn't matter: they knew I was a thief.

After about nine months, they returned me to reform school. My parole agent didn't think I had made much progress. He felt the attempt was a waste of time, primarily because of my attitude. But I hadn't been arrested, a point in my favor. The fact that there wasn't a policeman for twenty miles may have played a part in my "clean" record, though.

Reform school hadn't changed. This was the third time I had been there, so I felt like I knew my way around pretty well. They took me to the dining hall (where my cottage-mates were having lunch). Afterwards, just as we were about to leave for the cottage, I noticed a kind of weird-looking guy; and I was staring at him. He saw me looking at him and asked me if I had a problem. I told him, "Yeah, you," playing the role of someone who had been around. He just looked hard at me and said nothing. The procedure of entering the cottages was for the "belt" to go down the stairs with the keys, unlock the door, and count

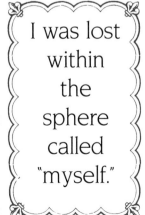

I was lost within the sphere called "myself."

the boys as they came in and then stood at attention until released by the staff who would enter the cottage last. As I entered, the weird-looking guy began hitting me with the buckle end of a belt wrapped around his hand. It came so quickly that I didn't have any time to protect myself. I got hit about eight times. I counted the bleeding welts later. I had to pretend nothing happened as the staff entered the cottage. If we weren't standing at attention in front of our assigned lockers when he entered, he would want to know why. I remember how hard it was to hide the pain and keep back the tears. But I wasn't going to "wimp out." I found out later this guy I had been staring at was a real bad ass, and he made up for his *feelings* of inadequacy by kicking butt. I stayed away from him; the situation was never mentioned again. The pecking order had been established.

This time back, they assigned me to a grounds crew. We did all the cleanup and the dirty work that no one else wanted to do. I spent about six weeks digging holes with a pick and shovel. It was late summer, and I could think of many things I would rather be doing. I had developed an interest in girls by now, but hadn't had a chance to meet anyone due to my restricted movements. Weekends in reform school were spent writing letters—if you had anyone to write to—shooting the bull with a buddy, or just lying around. It was not a real productive place. On Sunday afternoons we would see a movie. It was a time for mentally escaping this place. I remember becoming so interested in the movie that I would forget where I was until it got over. When I realized where I was, it hit with a sudden sad awareness.

This time I was in reform school about two months, and then they told me I would be given another chance at home with my family. I don't think they knew what else to do with me. I was not a behavior problem when I was in reform school, so they could not justify keeping me any longer. I didn't have any confidence in their decision. Things had not changed at home, and I had not changed for the better during the time I was gone. Quite the opposite: I had continued stealing, learned more about manipulating people, and had a very poor attitude. I thought I knew what was best for myself, and I didn't want anyone telling me what to do. I had picked up additional information on how to burglarize homes, steal cars, con people, and I had even began sniffing glue to get high while I was at reform school. They were not able to watch all of us all of the time. I had received my education all right, and now I would work at perfecting what I had learned.

I was prepared for the "free" world. But I soon discovered they were not prepared for me, nor were they prepared to put up with my anti-social behavior.

I was released in October of 1963. I was going to be home for Thanksgiving and Christmas for the first time in three years. I was 15 years old. The holidays were not what I had hoped for, and I found myself in constant turmoil with my father when he was around. My parents' relationship had gone downhill. The entire situation dete-

> The light at the end of all my tunnels faded, and went out as I grew older.

riorated to a point where my father would just come and go as he pleased. It was not an environment for positive growth.

I made it through the holidays without being arrested, but just barely. After Christmas, I ran away from home and committed some burglaries to support myself. I was suspected of doing some of those burglaries, so my parole agent told me I had violated the conditions of my parole, and he was taking me to a new facility for juvenile offenders. But in the meantime, until he could get free, I spent my time in a jail cell.

In January, 1964, they took me to Lino Lakes Reception and Diagnostic Treatment Center. It had an impressive name, but I knew it would be the same old thing: locked doors and limited privileges. Still, I was a little surprised by what I found. This place was new, clean, had good food, and there were girls there!

The girls' area opened first and had operated for about a

month, so there were about thirty girls there. I arrived the first day it opened for boys. There were only three of us boys there that first day; we liked the odds. Unfortunately, the only time of the day we could see the girls was during school when we would attend classes with them. On occasional Friday nights we would get together to talk and dance, our socialization process.

> Evil doesn't take days off.

I was only there for about six weeks, but it wasn't too bad a place. I fell for a girl who had been sent there for running away from home. So did another boy in my cottage, so we ended up in about three fights while I was there. It was nice to have girls around, but the resulting conflicts were evidence that this probably was not a good idea.

I went in front of the parole board, and they decided to send me to a youth forestry camp in northern Minnesota. That was about the last place I wanted to be. It was in the middle of nowhere, and there were not any girls for miles. To make matters worse, it was the dead of winter; and these guys worked outside cutting trees and clearing brush. I felt like my life was becoming more and more hopeless. I couldn't even understand why I was alive. What was the point of all this hell?

6

Do not let your vision be obscured by the shadows.

"IG JOHN" CAME DOWN FROM NORTH-ern Minnesota to pick us up; three of us were being sent to the forestry camp. Big John was, needless to say, big! He looked like a lumber-jack; he talked rough like a lumberjack too, but he turned out to be an OK guy. He told us about the camp on the four-hour drive up there. He made it sound all right. We would be going to school at the camp. The teachers came in from surrounding towns. In the afternoons, we would go out to the woods to cut and trim trees and brush. Weekends they took us to a gymnasium in the closest town so we could play basketball. If our work record was good, we would be able to see two movies a month. They took us into town on a big bus to the theater where we were all required to sit together. Big John told us if we "towed the line," it wouldn't be too bad a place.

We got there about 5 o'clock in the afternoon. As if to greet us, the snow was blowing and drifting; and it was well below zero. We could barely see the buildings as we drove into the camp. We were in the middle of a blizzard. We got settled that night and were told the rules we had to follow. We were allowed to smoke cigarettes whenever we wanted as long as we stayed in the "smok-ing areas." Smoking was a highly valued privilege. If we violated the rules, we lost our option to smoke, purely a control device. But I didn't hear anyone complaining. This problem with my smoking had begun with my father. Many of these boys had come into reform school or "the system" as non-smokers, and became smok-ers because it was set up as as a reward and there wasn't anything else to do. It was extremely easy to be caught up in the peer pressure to smoke. It was considered tough, and we liked to think of ourselves as tough guys. If a boy was weak or meek, he could count on being preyed upon by the bullies in the group who were ever-present.

A buddy I had known in Red Wing Reform School was there when I arrived, that cheered me up a little. We had spent some time together, and it was nice to see a familiar face. The first thing he asked me was if I wanted to run away with him that night. He and a couple of other guys had decided to make a break for it in the middle of the storm; they thought it would help cover their tracks. He was an Indian and had grown up in the north woods. He figured he could make it. I thought he was nuts! I tried to talk him out of it for two reasons: I never thought he would survive in the storm, and I didn't want the only real friend I had in this place to disappear. They left anyway. They were only gone about twenty minutes before someone noticed them missing. Extra staff members were called in to search for them. They had experienced enough runaways. They knew if they went to one of the areas the boys had to pass through and just sat there quietly, eventually the boys would be passing by. They brought them back, riding in the back of a pickup truck, after about three hours. They had already been out in below zero temperatures, and then they made them ride in the freezing winds in the back of that truck. I knew my buddy wished he had listened to me then. They were handcuffed to their beds that night as they slept; and in the morning, they were returned to Red Wing Reform School. I decided then and there that I wouldn't be attempting to run away. It obviously wasn't a very good idea.

The camp sat on a small hill surrounded by a thick forest. Most of the buildings appeared to be old army barracks, but there were some fairly new buildings. The dining hall was one of these. A big A-frame building, it was the center of activity. There were about forty boys at the camp at any given time. We worked hard and ate lots of food. Feeding forty hard-working, growing boys, took some big meals. The food was great compared to reform school, and the cooks knew it. Of all the staff in the camp; they were probably the most popular.

Our school was in a solid concrete building. Classes were the most boring part of the day for me. In spite of the below zero temperatures that were common, I would much rather have been outside working than sitting in that classroom, and I knew most of the other boys felt that way. One thing we had in common was our contempt for school. It was boring and took away time we could have used in ways that we thought would have been more fun. It is too bad that those activities we chose for ourselves were not more positive and fruitful.

I got into a couple of fights while I was at camp. The first was at school with a fellow in my class. I don't remember what it was about, but you can be sure pride played a part in it. We went at it for a few seconds, and I was getting the better of him when he grabbed a chair and swung it at me. He caught me in the left shoulder and hurt me badly (I still have an indentation of the chair's metal leg in my left shoulder). He lost his home visit, which was scheduled for the following week, for getting into a fight. Home visits were precious, you had to earn them by good behavior, acquiring days at the rate of one per month. But you could not take those days until you had a minimum of five days. You didn't see freedom for five months, and then you got only five days. A home visit happened only once during a boy's entire stay at the camp. I had expected the fellow to take out his anger on me—in his shoes, I know I would have. It was a very big deal. But he never approached me again.

> Ignorance is merely the door through which evil enters, accompanied by pride, evil's most constant companion.

After a big lunch, we would go back to the barracks and have a smoke and just shoot the bull. After about a half an hour, we would pile on a bus to the woods. Sometimes we worked miles from the camp, so it gave us more free time to smoke and exchange stories of our youthful adventures. The bull rode pretty high on those bus trips. Once we got to the woods, we would begin clearing brush. We had to clear the snow away from the base of the brush or trees before we could cut them. That year, there was about four feet of snow on the ground, so it was not an easy task. As we cleared brush, we would pile it in the middle of our work area and start burning it—to get rid of it, and for the warmth it provided. At break time, we would toast sandwiches the cook had given us for a snack. We learned quickly that you had to keep working at a steady clip to stay warm. We accomplished a lot of work in the four or five hours we were out in the woods. Then it was time for the bus ride back to camp where supper was waiting. We spent the rest of the evening playing cards, shooting pool, or watching television. It was very routine and extremely confining, certainly for teenagers.

The growth of a child ceases without nourishment.

The second fight I got into was with a guy who enjoyed bullying people. He pushed me too far, and I went after him. He wasn't expecting it, and I got in a few good punches before the staff came in and broke it up. He never tried to pick on me again. As a matter of fact, he came up to me the next day and apologized for messing with me; we ended up as friends. We had both learned something.

After I had been there for five months, I was scheduled for my home visit. I was really looking forward to that. Luckily I didn't lose it by fighting. They knew the guy was asking for it; he had a reputation for being a bully. The night before I was to leave for my home visit, they let me stay up as long as I wanted. I remember thinking that privilege was a pretty big deal (it was lights out at ten o'clock each night). I thought I'd stay up until two or three in the morning, because I was so wound up about going home, but I lasted only until midnight. I couldn't keep my eyes open.

The next morning they gave me a ride to town and a bus ticket along with the meager earnings I had accumulated during my five-month stay. They paid us 60 cents a day for our work in the forest, three dollars a week. This money paid for our cigarettes and candy bars which we could order once a month. The bus ride was long, and it seemed like forever. I had been stuck in the boonies hundreds of miles from nowhere.

When I got to the bus depot in St. Cloud, I was surprised to see my brother and some other people who had come to greet me. Their presence gave me a nice feeling I didn't experience very often.

My home visit was spent pleasantly enough. My father was pretty much gone from the home now, so I did what I wanted. It was at this time that I had my first sexual experience with a girl, searching for closeness and love.

My five days of freedom passed very quickly. It seemed like I had just gotten off the bus and it was time to get back on it. So I decided to get on a different bus, going to Minneapolis. I had a buddy who had told me to come and see him if I was ever on "the run" and needed a place to stay. But when I got there, his parents wouldn't even let him talk to me, let alone consider having me as a guest. I found a crawl space under some stairs in an apartment building somewhere in northeast Minneapolis. I stashed my suitcase there and wandered around the city just out of boredom, going back to my crawl space to sleep.

I soon ran out of money, and things became a little less boring. I went to Dayton's Department Store and charged some clothes to my parents' account with a credit card I had taken from my mother's purse while I was home. I got out of the store; but as I switched my IDs in my billfold, (I had a fake one) a plain-clothes detective from the store grabbed me. He had suspected something was wrong and kept an eye on me, and saw me switch IDs.

To prove my identity, I had to give them my father's phone number at his law office. He told them I could keep the clothes, but he also told them I was on the run from the law. They contacted the police, and I was soon in the Hennepin County Jail to be held until I could be transported back to Lino Lakes Reception Center to appear before the parole board for escape.

The parole board didn't waste a lot of time. They told me I would return to reform school, and they would see me in another three months. This was my fourth stay at Red Wing Reform School; I had just turned 16 years old.

At reform school, they assigned me to the cottage that was in charge of the dining room. Our job was to help the cooks prepare the meals, serve the other boys as they passed along the food line with their trays, and wash and put away the trays and silverware afterward. It was considered a good cottage to be in because we had free time between meals. There were other advantages: we ate very well and often had access to extra food and we got extra cigarettes. In all of the other cottages, they received only four cigarettes a day. In ours, we would get up to eight a day.

A few weeks after I had been there, and had settled into the routine, a boy arrived from my hometown. I didn't know him, but he came up to me and pretended we were buddies. He was very naive, and, no doubt, scared to death. But I knew if I teamed up with this guy, or had anything to do with him, I would be considered just as simple and naive. I didn't care for him anyway. If he had sat quietly in a corner somewhere, he would have been left alone. But he was trying to be buddies with everyone, making a real clown of himself, which is a poor beginning in such a hostile environment as reform school.

Unfortunately for him, it was shower night; and all of us had to shower and get fresh clothes. We had a big shower room with no supervision. Some bullies surrounded him and told him it was initiation time, and he had to perform oral sex on them. At first he hesitated, but the others punched and kicked him until he agreed. He got down on his knees, and the whole crowd around him kicked and beat him until he could not get up. They left the shower laughing. I didn't see any humor in the situation.

This kid finally got to his feet and looked at me with tears and blood running down his face, and said he didn't know it was going to be like this. He said he would never be able to take it. Pushed just a step further, he would have been a prime candidate for suicide. I told him the best thing to do was keep his mouth shut and keep to himself. He followed my advice. I don't recall him ever approaching me to talk again.

He was one boy I knew would never return to reform school. He was very much affected by his experiences and he probably never did another thing wrong in his life. I felt sorry for him; but if I had intervened, I would have probably been treated the same way. You do not take on the power structure; you adapt. I could relate very easily to some of the feelings he was having. This was the first time he had been separated from his family and home, and such a memory stays with a young boy. If he had allowed the feelings of loneliness and hopelessness to overwhelm him, the officials might as well take him out of reform school in a strait jacket and commit him to a state mental hospital. I've seen that happen on occasion. People who have never experienced such intense feelings can in no way understand the depth into which these cause the human mind to sink. So the "prisoner" must become flexible or he will shatter like a pane of glass.

The Lost and Lonely

I see them
in the shadows,
in their windows
late at night.
They move with emptiness;
with less a sense of purpose,
than out of habit.
Waiting for that moment
when they will cast a shadow
upon this earth no more,
and where this becomes
just another place
they have been.

Written at Red Wing Reform School, 1964.

7 The combination of ignorance and evil is a very dangerous one.

ELEASED FROM REFORM SCHOOL, I returned home in the fall of 1964. I made it through the holidays with my family again. My father wasn't around much. They sent me back to reform school shortly after the new year because I refused to stay at home most of the time. In my need for money, I committed several more burglaries.

I do not recall much "free time" in my teenage years. I was caught in a cycle because of my behavior; and because of my behavior and attitude, no one really wanted to help. One thing that made the situation worse was that I felt I had all the answers and would refuse to cooperate with anyone who tried to help me. Many psychologists and psychiatrists interviewed me. It seemed they would talk to me for a while, and I would leave their office with them shaking their heads in exasperation. I didn't have much regard for the ideas of others, and it showed.

They put me into the same cottage I had been in the last time I was there. I hadn't been gone long, so there were still some of the boys there I had known before. I knew a lot of the boys in the other cottages. A lot of us just kept coming back.

As soon as I arrived, they asked me if I wanted the job of hospital "belt." I would have the responsibility of escorting boys from the hospital area back to their cottages or job. The staff knew me well enough to trust me with that kind of a job. I had never had any significant trouble in my stays there. It was a good job; I had a lot of freedom.

I went before the parole board about two months after I

had been back. They said I was doing a good job, but they thought I might benefit more from another forestry camp that was hidden somewhere in the most northern part of Minnesota. I told them I would like to go there. We were allowed to smoke cigarettes anytime we wanted at the forestry camps; that privilege was incentive enough for me. So in the early winter of 1965, they transferred me to another camp in the middle of nowhere, located on a lake. I liked the setting because I really enjoyed fishing, one of the few things my father and I had done together. Beside the lake, we were surrounded by huge pine trees with many paths leading into the woods. This place had potential. I thought I might even get to like it, but not until winter was over. We arrived in the middle of a big blizzard with temperatures of around ten below zero, and there was no school here. We spent our entire day in the forest cutting trees and brush.

Our routine was much the same as it was at the previous camp. There were about forty boys in this camp, which was constructed of old army barracks. On the really cold and windy days, I can still remember the ice that would form on the inside of certain weak spots on the buildings. It didn't bother us much, since we considered ourselves rugged. We worked hard in the woods, and we were proud of what we accomplished as a group. We took pride in our ability to unify ourselves when an extra effort was needed. Sometimes on our trips in the bus, we would come upon someone who had slid off the road or was stuck in a ditch full of snow. The driver of the bus would pull over, and we would all pile out, surround the car, and lift it right out of the ditch. People would look on in amazement at our efforts. I'm sure some people were surprised at our enthusiasm to help others; it's not the kind of picture you generally get of juvenile delinquents. But the majority of us were not bad kids, we were confused, lonely; and, for the most part, we felt abandoned. The camaraderie we had was, for many of us, our first experience with shared responsibility and its rewards. We needed that positive input in our lives. I have to admit, I learned to work in that camp. I understood what the word meant when I left there.

When spring finally arrived, we could hear the woods becoming filled with more and more sounds of life. The ice went off the lake and we would watch shimmering sunsets reflected in the lake. We were able to wander in the woods, fish or swim, or just lie around when we weren't working. It was not too bad, considering its counterparts.

We had a few strange boys among us. One boy in particular built a little prison out of rocks he found by the lake. He would catch frogs and snakes and "lock them up" in separate areas. Then he would release the frogs into the snake area, and the snakes would eat the frogs. But it didn't stop there. After they had eaten the frogs, you could see the bulge in the snake's body where the frog was. He would squeeze the frog out of the snake, and set the frog free again, out "on parole." Then he would capture more frogs the next day and repeat the process. He called this place "Alca-Frog."

He was somewhat entertaining, but I kept my distance from him. Usually you find just one person like that in a crowd, here you might find a dozen. Some were humorous, some were downright dangerous. You learned to stay alert.

I developed an ear infection and was taken to the nearest town with a doctor to have my ear checked on a Friday afternoon. Waiting in his office, I dug through the drawers in his desk. I found a bottle of Phenobarbital capsules and put it in my pocket. I knew it was something I could get high on. I had heard the other boys discussing drugs and I remembered the name of the drug. When I got back to the barracks, I took three of the capsules. I didn't knew much about drugs then, but I had heard enough from others to make me curious. The pills made me feel pretty high, so I took some more thinking I would feel higher. I got higher all right: I know I came very close to overdosing. I took about eight or ten of those pills during the afternoon and evening. I woke up Saturday morning at 11 a.m. with the biggest headache I had ever had, and I felt drugged and sick throughout the day. A buddy of mine who had some common sense took the pills and threw them away. At first I was mad; but in looking back, I realize that he may have saved my life.

The only time I got caught doing anything wrong was an incident involving a spear I made. I found an old butcher knife in the woods. The handle was beginning to rot off. I removed the remainder of the handle and got a long bamboo fishing pole. I fastened the blade to the large end of the fishing pole with some wire and some heavy tape I had found, and had a mighty fancy spear.

I would check out to wander in the woods and go get my spear from where I had hidden it. I never used it for hunting, although it would have been easy enough. There were beaver, raccoon, and newborn fawns all through the woods. I would just practice throwing it at trees and other targets just for fun. It fed my sense of adventure. It was fun to pretend I lived alone in the woods and had to hunt my food and watch out for any signs of danger. I was still a kid and lived in a kid's world. But I went to the woods a little too often, so the staff decided to check on me. These guys were brought up in the woods, and they were sneaky. Someone followed me to see what I was up to. He saw me throwing the spear. When I headed back to camp, I put it in my usual hiding spot. He went looking for the spear, but he couldn't find it, so he came back to camp, confronted me and told me to go and get the spear and bring it to him. It was no wonder he couldn't find it. I would just stick it in the ground next to a tree so it blended right in, and there were an awful lot of trees in that forest. I would remember where I had hidden it, but for someone to go out there looking for a piece of wood in a forest is like trying to find a needle in a haystack. I think I got punished more as a result of their anger at not being able to find my weapon than for having the spear. They made me split wood all day on a Saturday for that little escapade.

I was one of six boys selected to go and plant some trees on the edge of the Boundary Waters Canoe Area. Several troops of Boy Scouts had gathered for a massive effort to get several hundred thousand trees planted in a period of two days, to be followed by three days of camping and fishing. The six of us were told that if we hustled and did a good job, we would be allowed to participate in the camping and fishing activities. We got the work done in the two days as planned. With two boys to a canoe, they let us go across the lake and set up our camps for the next three days. We had to stay in sight of the staff, but that restriction was fine with us, since they were across the lake. So we fished and slept out under the stars. It was really a nice break, but it was just too short a time. We would have stayed there for the summer if they had let us. I must admit the thought of getting into a canoe and leaving entered my mind more than once. I loved the woods and the lakes and the freedom they held for me. But the trip ended, and we went back to camp to tell the others about our adventures.

When I was close to being released, my father came up to the camp to visit me. He said I could come and live with him when I got out. Then he started laying down the rules; he wanted to control my every move. I resented his interference very much. I hadn't even had my childhood. That was gone. I just wish he would lighten up and give me a break; all I wanted was to be a happy kid. Here I was in the spring of my 17th year of life. I had been in Red Wing Reform School five times, two different forestry camps, several jails, and a foster home—all in about four-and-a-half years. I wondered what happened to my life. I knew I was not a terrible person, just very confused, lonely, and at a complete loss when it came to a reason to live. I was sick of people shuffling me around. I told my father he could take his rules and shove them. I was tired of constantly having to give in to authority figures.

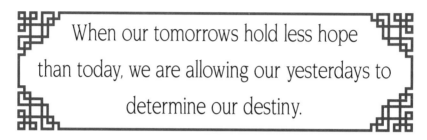

When our tomorrows hold less hope than today, we are allowing our yesterdays to determine our destiny.

He drove away angry as hell, and I went back into the barracks. I didn't care if I had lost an opportunity to get out. It seemed it didn't make a lot of difference where I was; the end result was the same anyway. I would have been happy to go and live with my mother at that time, but she had the other five children and she didn't feel she could handle me. I have to admit, I could not blame her: she had enough to worry about without me there to drive her crazy with my behavior. My parents' divorce was final, and she was now alone trying to raise five school-age children. None of the kids would—or could—deal with my father, so my mother had the responsibility of trying to instill good values and growth into their lives.

This was the mid 1960s: many things were changing. It was a turbulent time for a young person. The war in Viet Nam was in full swing. Drugs were becoming available in the city of St. Cloud; before, you had to go to Minneapolis to look for them. Bob Dylan sang, "The times, they are a-changing," and they were indeed.

My father and I finally reached a compromise that I felt I could live with, at least until I got out of the forestry camp. And that is just about how long the arrangement worked. Within two weeks of getting out of the camp, I was back living with my mother. She would never turn me away, but I know it was not easy for her. I had a terrible temper, and I did just as I pleased. I came and went without even an exchange of words.

I was very fortunate she *was* my mother: no one else would

have put up with me. She did demonstrate a good example for me; she was kind, considerate, sensitive and unselfish. I haven't met many people like her in my life. I learned the majority of people were not like her at all, but the exact opposite!

I've been disenchanted with people since I began to recognize the contradiction between their words and their behavior. I was sucked in by the words in the beginning. I was taught the world was basically good and fair with the opportunity for real happiness. I would have appreciated being told the truth instead of having to spend so much of my time reacting to those lies. One psychiatrist laughed at me and said I was foolishly idealistic in expecting people to live good, honest lives and follow God's commandments. I may have been idealistic, but I was not wrong in expecting people to practice what they preach. When I learned that a lot of people didn't play by the rules, then I decided I wouldn't, either. In my own lost way, I continued to search for something to believe in.

I was only home about six weeks before I found myself in trouble again. A fellow I knew asked me where he could get some money. I said I would tell him, but I wanted a share of it. He agreed and I told him about a place where they kept the cash under a counter in a cigar box. It was a small business where the owner was in and out of the back room a lot, so your timing had to be good. I knew it was risky (too risky for me at the time). But I had filed it away in case something came up. He got the money and gave me a share, but then he got caught, and told the police I had given him the necessary information. He went to court and got put on probation—no big deal for him.

Because of my history and reputation, they bound me over to municipal court as an adult (I had just turned 17 years old). They charged me with aiding-and-abetting in theft. I pled guilty, thinking the judge might go easier on me. He gave me 90 days in the county jail. Another summer locked up. So, I assembled a bunch of books and spent the majority of my time reading, since there wasn't anything else to do. I had been writing from time to time in my life, mostly poetry. It seemed necessary to express myself in some way; I had no one to talk to about my feelings. Most of my poems told of emptiness, sadness, and longing; they were not inspiritional material. I would think about how much I was missing being locked up in jail again. It seemed that my entire life had been spent either in reform school and jails, or else on the run from the police. I felt that I held very little value at that time of my life.

They released me from jail near the end of summer. I

The old Stearns County Jail, 1960s.

PHOTOS (THIS PAGE AND NEXT) COURTESY OF STEARNS COUNTY
SHERIFF'S DEPT.

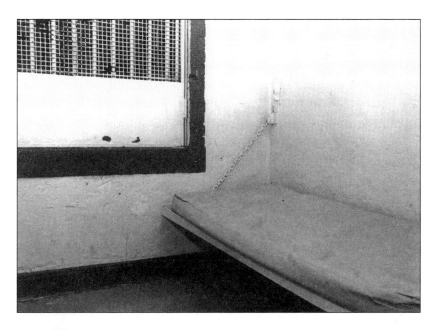

Typical confinement cell, Stearns County Jail, 1960s. No frills, no diversions, no entertainment—but plenty of time for serious reflection!

began spending a great deal of my time sniffing glue to get high. The solvent, toluene, would put me into a sort of trance-like state. I would be caught up in hallucinations. It was as though I was transported to another place—a safer, kinder and gentler place, which was extremely attractive. I didn't like the real world very much.

Occasionally, I would wander through my mother's house with a bag full of glue in my hand, making my mother, my brothers and sisters very uncomfortable. I guess the reason they didn't call the police was because they knew the authorities would only lock me up again. I think everyone hoped I would just snap out of it some day.

After a while, one of my sisters moved out of the house we were living in. She had a bedroom on the second story of the house with windows looking out over the street below, and I moved in there. I was sniffing glue one day; and as I looked out the window, I could see the children playing in the street below, laughing and having fun. I was suddenly filled with the thought that I was retarded and I was being kept away from others because of it. There was something wrong with me, and I didn't fit in. My refuge was inside myself.

For several months, I continued to sniff glue on a daily basis. I knew sniffing glue killed brain cells. I don't know how much damage was done. Considering the amounts of glue that I sniffed and the frequency, I should be dead.

It wasn't long before other drugs became much more available to me. They were safer than the glue and more appealing as well.

8 A crisis is a bus stop to God.

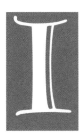I MET MY FIRST WIFE ABOUT THIS TIME. She was beautiful, young, innocent, and a very sensitive person. We had a lot of fun together. But we were both so young that our judgment was not the best. She became pregnant, so we decided to get married. I had just turned eighteen, but she was only seventeen; so she needed her parents' permission. They very reluctantly signed the necessary papers allowing her to get married, and we moved in together.

The plan was for her to complete her senior year at high school, and I was going to get a job and support us. I proved to be totally unreliable. I couldn't keep a job; I would always find something wrong with it. Whether it was the people I worked with or just the job itself, I always had an excuse for not working. I simply did not want to work; I wanted to have fun.

I was also very aware of feeling lonely when I was away from my wife. I was very insecure.

We separated before the baby was even born. My wife filed for divorce and we were divorced after we had been married only seven months. She wanted to give the child up for adoption because she knew she wasn't ready for the responsibility of raising a child. She wanted to continue her education. I objected to the adoption initially, but I was talked into it and signed the papers that gave up my rights as a parent. I didn't like it, but I knew it was best. I was not prepared to take on the responsibility of raising a child, either. I was still a child myself. Following is a poem about my first wife I wrote years later while in prison:

Suzanne Through Eternity

Although with peace I bid you farewell,
Within my heart you shall be evermore;
For there is no flower without the seed,
Nor peace without the threat of war.

I shall remember then, the flower,
And cherish each and every spring;
When at the warmth it brings, you bloom,
And through the fields your beauty rings.

As the sweetness on the lips which lingers,
After tasting nature's fresh pure fruits;
So shall you sweetly linger on,
And sweeten my life with thoughts of you.

A child you were when I came upon you,
A child forever you shall be;
There is nothing more innocent or pure,
Than that which you have been to me.

Together we have lived a life,
Reborn within a single soul;
But as all things become reborn,
The life of death shall take its toll.

Written in prison, 1970.

When I was with my wife, I had used alcohol, speed, and a few barbiturates. Shortly after our divorce, I began to experiment with anything I could get my hands on: a journey of exploration, a trip through my mind and body. I used everything from class A narcotics (the very addictive and controlled drugs—delaudid, morphine, demoral, cocaine, etc.), to LSD and marijuana. My addictions significantly slowed the normal maturation process. In effect, I had stopped growing, stopped learning, and eventually I would stop caring about anything except getting the drugs I needed to shoot in my veins.

An acquaintance of mine had discovered some drugs his father had put away before he died. His father had been a doctor; and judging from what this kid found, he may have been an addict, too. There were bottles and bottles of Class A narcotics which had never been opened, with the tax stamp still in place. There was pharmaceutical cocaine, and vials of morphine. Altogether, there were two old doctors' bags filled with drugs. The first thing I ever injected into my veins was cocaine. I will never forget the rush of the drug through my system. It was simply beyond description. If I had to make a choice between sex or cocaine, at that time, I would have chosen the cocaine, no question about it.

As it was, I didn't have to make that choice. It was 1968. The hippie movement was in full swing along with the free love that went with it. I was very promiscuous and moved from girl to girl without much thought about it.

Around this time, I began carrying a gun because of my drug use and paranoia. The drug world could be a dangerous place.

Every young person I knew then was experimenting with drugs. That may have been because I hung around with a particular crowd, but I don't necessarily think so; it seemed like everyone wanted to experiment with marijuana and LSD. Drugs were abundant and what we could not find on the streets, we would steal or forge prescriptions for.

I never had a job that lasted more than a few days. Crime and dealing drugs were my income.

The police were called to my mother's house on numerous

occasions. If I was yelling at my mother, my younger brothers sometimes called the police because they were afraid I might hurt her. (I never did.) Or if I got into an argument with one of my brothers, they would call the police out of fear of escalation. On one of these occasions I was arrested for possession of marijuana. The police talked my mother into signing a complaint against me for disorderly conduct because of my behavior. They had done that more than once. After they had me handcuffed, they searched my bedroom and found a couple of ounces of pot. This was a big deal to them; they hadn't had many drug arrests in St. Cloud. My bail was set at $5000. It was 1968, and the punishment for possession of marijuana was 0-20 years in prison.

My father wouldn't bail me out of jail for a while. He thought it might teach me a lesson. *That's just what I needed, another lesson!*—but it was typical of my father's reasoning. After an attorney was appointed to represent me in the case, my father agreed to help with the bail. I was back using drugs immediately after my release from jail.

> Ignorance is a puddle we all must pass through; it is unfortunate that some of us get caught in the storm itself.

My attorney was able to set the date for the trial a couple of months down the road, so I had some free time. I didn't think they were going to send me to prison for possession of marijuana, so I didn't worry about it. I figured I'd get a slap on the wrist and be put on probation for a few years. I continued down that same road I had chosen for myself. I was approaching a dead end, but I did not know that then.

I had become addicted to the needle. It didn't matter what drug I was injecting, I loved the "rush" that would come when the drug suddenly hit your system. I had a friend who was in much the same state of mind. We would get the home addresses of doctors and go out about three o'clock in the morning to rip off the emergency medicine they kept in their little black bags. We would almost always find the bag in their cars, which meant it wasn't necessary to enter anything but the garage. It was like taking candy from a baby.

No one knew how much the problem of drugs was going to escalate. I knew sons and daughters of some of the most prominent citizens of St. Cloud who injected drugs regularly. No one was immune to the effects of this stuff. One shot in the arm and your life could be changed forever. My friend and I had accumulated piles of drugs. We used a Physician's Desk Reference, a book that identifies drugs and their uses and side affects to identify the drugs we had stolen. There were times when we would not find the drug we were seeking information about, and we would just inject the drug to see what the effects were—a move which was downright stupid, but we didn't care. We were "hooked."

By the time I was 20 years old, I had used LSD, marijuana, cocaine, morphine, dilaudid, Demerol, peyote, crystal methedrine, and many sedatives and barbiturates. I was hooked on a high. It didn't matter what it was: getting high controlled my behavior. I conned and manipulated people to get what I wanted and needed. I measured their value only by what I could get from them to help myself deeper into my addiction.

> I sought enchantment at every fork in the road. My mistake was in allowing my body, instead of God's will, to choose my path.

Using LSD changed the way I looked at things. I was continually amazed at what I saw and felt. I became much more aware of the potential of the mind; and it was incredible. You hear about how we only use about one-tenth of the brain. This is very evident after you have experienced LSD. My perception of myself and my surroundings began to change. I became more and more interested in the existence of a spiritual world and the possibilities that lay beyond that. LSD truly opened doors. The problem, however, was sometimes these doors didn't swing shut at the end of the "trip."

After awhile, it became evident the effects of drugs were taking their toll. I knew several people who had died of drug overdoses. They were all addicts who used heavy drugs like heroin, dilaudid, or morphine. I had a friend my age who got killed in a shoot-out when he was trying to rip off some drug dealers. I had still another friend who had suffered serious effects from LSD. LSD was, in fact, an induced psychosis. One of my friends had a "bad trip" and couldn't quite get back. He got stuck someplace else and was never the same person at all. LSD is a powerful drug, capable of taking you places you have never imagined. It was not something to be taken lightly or without preparation, both physical and psychological.

I had numerous acquaintances who were either in jail, a treatment center, or prison. Everyone around me was being affected by drug use, and not in a good way.

Once, I was at a party where drugs were being used freely by everyone attending. Some people were smoking pot, and others were injecting cocaine and other drugs. I was carrying a gun (a 25-automatic) that I wanted to sell, and some guy asked to see it. I showed it to him several times (always removing the clip beforehand). He asked to see it once more; I warned him that it was loaded. As he leaned over to look at it in the light, he pulled the trigger. The bullet passed through his hand and into the ceiling. In his drugged stupor, he forgot that it was loaded.

When he went to the hospital, the doctor called the police. The police tried to get him to say I shot him, since I had a bad reputation, and they figured that was what happened. But he convinced them he was telling the truth—or at least that he was going to stick to his story. Each of us was being affected by the use of drugs. There were about 30 people at that party. It would have been just as easy for someone to have been hit in the head with that bullet, and died. Common sense went right out the window with drug use. But the escape the drugs provided had changed our priorities.

When I entered the twentieth year of my life, I had been shooting a lot of cocaine into my arms. I was in love with this drug. My life was this drug, and it was the only relationship I had.

Continued injections of cocaine will eventually lead to a very powerful paranoia. The same thing happens with speed or methedrine. Because it produces such intensely good feelings, you tend to overlook the fact that you must eat and take in nourishment to maintain your mind and body. That lack of nourishment affects your thinking. It was important to be aware of that condition. I had friends whom I had seen coming down from drugs, and they believed they were being followed, surrounded by the police, or in some immediate danger. I needed to have some sedatives or tranquilizers when I began to come down from the drugs. It was a process of getting what I could and shooting it until it was gone, usually three or four days. Then I would come down to get some sleep and eat some food, only to get up and do it again. If this process is allowed to continue, the end result is the loss of your mind or your life. There are no other choices.

When I ran out of cocaine, I'd shoot crystal methedrine, speed. But I had to continue to steal to get the money I would need for my drug use. I ripped off drug dealers whenever I had the opportunity. They always had cash and drugs, but it was risky business. I was pretty brazen, I was street wise, all drugged up, or desperate for some drugs, and carried a gun. I told people who had problems with me they better get themselves a gun if they were going to pursue the issue because that was the level at which we would be working. I had some close calls, but generally came out all right. I really didn't care if I lived or died. My life was valueless.

The police were aware of some of my activities and were just waiting to put me away. But there was so much drug use going on they were kept real busy. They were initially overwhelmed by the sudden influx of drugs into the community. It happened very fast and it spread like wildfire. It took the parents of the children by surprise as well. Most of them didn't notice much in the beginning. But as their child's drug use went from marijuana to LSD and on to speed or cocaine, or to morphine or heroin, then they would notice when money and valuables disappeared and their child's behavior changed.

The following poem is an indication of my dismal outlook during this period of my life.

It's Mine

Stones spread over a desolate land,
life's troubles departed, all was planned.
Trees flow sadly in the frozen breeze,
and gone is the blood red love we tried to seize.

Our next step takes us to a path; it's time.
A concerned action forgotten, it's mine.
I stand alone near a solid stone gate,
I reach to touch, but alas too late,
it, too, departs with time.
A life forgotten, it's mine.

Open earth, unto you I'm thrown,
Ah, it's proper, for on you I've grown.
And the people screamed and raved,
prophetized and prayed,
of course, with time,
For beneath them lies a grave;
It's mine.........

Written in prison, 1969.

I knew quite a few people in Minneapolis who used and sold drugs. Most of them I had known from my trips to Red Wing Reform School or one of the other "facilities" I had been locked up in. We were a real crazy group when we all got together—all using drugs of one sort or another, and all criminals. None of us worked for a living. Most of us carried guns, but even though we were high on dope, we never used those guns the way they are used today. Ours were strictly for protection from being ripped off by other drug users. If you could handle yourself well and carried a gun, people didn't mess with you.

I would go from St. Cloud down to Minneapolis and St. Paul to party, and sometimes I would take some of my friends down there with me. There was one person in particular that I was spending a lot of time with, and I had taken him down to the Twin Cities a few times. One time we had been down there together and I decided to go back to St. Cloud. He decided to stay down there, so I left. A couple of days later I got a phone call from one of my buddies in Minneapolis. He told me my friend had been stabbed to death the night before. Apparently he was at a party and was feeling pretty good. He had a tendency to be funny and laugh a lot and have fun in lots of situations. This time he carried it a little too far: he had approached a girl at the party and she gave him the brush-off. But when the girl left the party, he approached her again (it was just like him—he was persistent but funny). But the girl got scared and pulled a knife from her purse and stabbed him in the chest three times. He dropped to the side-walk and was dead before the ambulance got there.

The girl was a 15 year old runaway from Minneapolis. She had been drinking and using drugs at the party. I wouldn't want to carry around the guilt of having taken a life, especially when it is not something that would have happened had drugs and alcohol not been involved. The saddest

I discovered, in my search for truth, there is not a fine line between sanity and madness. There is, however, a bridge—an often traveled bridge.

thing about this situation was that he was one of the easiest going fellows I knew. He was always there with a joke or a good laugh. It was not necessary to be a bad person to be affected by what was happening around us. But we always think it won't happen to us.

Although it had not happened to me, it was close enough that I felt I could be next. Still I had the attitude it didn't matter. I wasn't especially happy with this place we call earth anyway. I wasn't the only one that was screwed up; the whole world was. All you had to do was read the paper or listen to the news. I didn't feel any of us had a chance the way things were going.

A Funeral

The insane people be,
One great wall surrounding me.
Like an island I shall lie,
Within this tomb, I shall die.

Lost like spring in winter's season,
Grasping for some unknown reason.
I sit and wait in solitude,
And end within ineptitude.

Fantasy sinks dark and deep,
And realism takes a front row seat.
I pause and wonder what is wrong,
And realize my life goes on.

A sacred arm surrounds my shoulders,
Within my heart my love, it smolders.
Burning deep within my soul,
Trying to find a lasting goal.

And as a man, I'll try to please,
And fall upon my bended knees.
Trying to make my God appear,
Hoping that he's standing near.

Then I know I've been misled,
I must be,
I have to be,
I am.........DEAD.

Written in prison, 1969.

The world was shot and going to hell anyway. I just wanted to make the decisions about what I would do until then. What was different about the way that I took things from others, compared to the way everyone else tried to screw their neighbor? A country, a people, or a corporation—it didn't matter who you examined. The bottom line was, everyone was using everyone else to their own advantage, including me. I was just a little more out front with it.

What made me different was my perception of that reality. I was deeply affected and disappointed that I didn't see goodness, love, trust, patience, and a "love-your-neighbor" attitude in those around me. It would have certainly made this world an easier place to adjust to. Why, then, should anyone expect anything different from *me* than what I was becoming?

I was again arrested for possession of marijuana, this time in the Minneapolis area. I got arrested with about six ounces of pot. When the court found out I had been arrested previously for the same offense, they decided to send me to Lino Lakes Reception Center, which was serving as a receiving area for the St. Cloud Reformatory. I had been at Lino Lakes about two weeks when I began having chest pains. I was taken to the hospital with my face wrapped in gauze, riding in the very back of a station wagon. The staff had been told by the hospital that it appeared from my X-rays it was very likely I had TB.

When I was arrested, I had been shooting speed for several months. I had not been eating any more than the minimum to keep me alive. I weighed 123 pounds and I was 6'2". I looked like the walking dead. There were definite similarities between how I looked and how I felt inside myself. I was 21 years old. I had failed to complete high school because I was expelled for fighting. I was addicted to drugs, and it looked like I was going to prison. At that point, I held little hope for myself. Instead of being filled with hopeful expectations for the future, I was filled with an indescribable loneliness, complete despair, and a lot of anger. 🕊

9 Conflict is not of God, resolution is.

OR FIVE WEEKS I WAS IN THE HOSPItal. It had been determined through biopsies that I had a disease called sarcoidosis. It was not a very common illness, and the doctors could not determine where I had come in contact with it. I think I was very susceptible to any illness at that time because of my degenerated condition.

The doctors prescribed steroids and rest. They gave me Talwin (synthethic morphine) every four hours for pain. So, in effect, I was still being injected with drugs. I had been given a medical parole so the State Corrections Department wouldn't have to bear the cost of my hospitalization. I thought that because of my illness, the parole board would be merciful with me and release me from the hospital. They decided instead to send me to St. Cloud Reformatory. I was going home, but not to my family, just to the city where my family lived.

I had seen the reformatory from the outside. It had huge granite walls, four feet thick and 22 feet high, surrounding it and looked like a fortress. But I had never seen it from the inside. Two sheriff's deputies transferred me from the hospital to the reformatory. As we got closer and closer to the reformatory and things began to look familiar, I decided I couldn't just let them take me there without an attempt to escape—I knew once I was inside those walls there would be no way out. So I pretended I was going to be sick and they pulled the car over to the side of the highway. Keep in mind, I was handcuffed and had been injected with drugs every four hours up until I went to the parole hearing. One of the deputies opened the back door of the car and then got back in the front seat. I got my feet out on the ground and hung my head, pretending I was going to get sick. As soon as I heard the deputies talking in the front seat and I thought they were distracted, I made a break for it. I got about six feet before I fell the first time. I struggled to get up and ran another six feet before I fell again. Because of my weakened condition, I was having trouble keeping my balance. On top of everything else, I hadn't been out of bed except to go to the bathroom in five weeks. I was struggling to get up again when the deputies grabbed me. I was completely exhausted, and I had only made it about twelve feet from the car. I don't know how I thought I could out-run two healthy deputies. My state of mind was as weak as my body.

When we got inside the walls of the reformatory, they told me to sit down and wait for processing. The deputies went into an office with another fellow and I thought they were going to tell him about my attempted escape. That offense carried an additional seven years on a prisoner's sentence and I had been sentenced to 0-20 years for possession of marijuana. But they felt so sorry for me that they decided not to tell anyone. It was no wonder they felt sorry for me, because I looked like a beaten man, inside and out. I barely spoke unless spoken to. While I sat there waiting to be processed, I saw many familiar faces in the inmate population. I recognized a lot of fellows from reform school, the forestry camps, and jails where I had been in off and on during all those years. It was like "old home" week: everyone was there. I was filled with dread at the thought of spending several years in that place.

I spent the first night at the reformatory in the infirmary. I had not been officially released from the hospital, so it was necessary to hold me in quarantine until I was examined by a physician the following day. I remember that dark little room they put me in. All it had in it was a metal bed, a sink, and a toilet. After dark, I could look out my window between the bars and see the huge walls that surrounded me, and I could hear the trains passing by outside the walls. I wished I was on one headed somewhere else. There was a rock quarry I used to swim in right on the other side of the walls. I remembered going there with some friends to swim, drink beer, and smoke pot when I was a few years younger. I also remembered telling someone with me at the time I would *never* be in this place, I had been so sure it would never happen. But as in everything else, I thought I had all the answers. I was discovering I had been wrong, very wrong.

The next morning a doctor examined me and released me from medical supervision. They put me into the general population and assigned me a cell. The cells were six by ten feet. There was a sink, a toilet, and a metal bed; the "room" I'd been in the night before was a suite compared to these.

They told me I would have to go through an orientation class before I was assigned to a permanent job placement. This orientation meant yet another series of tests. I considered them a complete waste of my time, but I complied, since I had no choice in the matter. In addition to the testing, I had interviews with a psychologist, a case worker, and a doctor. But I had grown used to people prodding and probing me—something which had been going on most of my life.

After about two weeks, they assigned me a job as a clerk in the engineer's office and moved me to another cell house: "A" house. There were five cell houses in the reformatory, each holding approximately 135 inmates. The cells are arranged in tiers, four high, just like in the movies. Our only source of "entertainment" was a pair of headphones we could plug into the wall to receive one of two outside radio stations piped in. We also had our own channel that was broadcast from inside the prison by inmates. It carried announcements, and we could make requests for a particular song to be played on the "inmate" station. The last thing I wanted to hear was music that would remind me of happier moments. It only made the situation more difficult. I kept to myself quite a bit those first few weeks. I was not in the mood to talk to anyone. I did a great deal of thinking about what was going to happen to my life, and it didn't look good.

My job assignment as a clerk was considered a good one. There were many people who could not read or write in the reformatory simply because they had not made it through school because of their delinquency problems. Despite my overall degenerated condition, I scored fairly high on the tests that I took to measure my intelligence and my reading and writing abilities.

The job was a piece of cake. There were two other clerks in the engineer's office, and barely enough work to keep one person busy. So, needless to say, we had a lot of free time. The construction office was adjacent to the engineer's office, and I became fast friends with an inmate who had been assigned there. With all the spare time we had, we could get passes from our supervisors and go pretty much where we wanted to go—within the walls, of course. The first week I was there, this buddy of mine and I got a pass to go down to the school area. We found a room that wasn't being used and we went in there. He pulled out a joint (marijuana cigarette) and I got my first taste of dope in prison. I was somewhat surprised at its availability in there, but I would soon learn you could get whatever you wanted—if you had the cash! Even though it was against the rules for any inmate to have cash, there was no shortage of it. An inmate could ask visitors very quietly and carefully to pass it to him in the visiting room or exchange cartons of cigarettes for cash with other inmates who had cash, usually those who sold drugs. So, here I was in prison for smoking pot, and any drug I wanted was still available to me. It didn't make much sense to me then, nor does it now. Drugs and money made up the majority of contraband smuggled into the prison by visitors and by some employees. Money talks, and it doesn't seem to matter where you are.

I was able to get a cell change to the same cell house where my buddy from the construction office was. My view of the outside changed: I had windows across from my cell that looked directly out to freedom. I could see the roads I had driven down when I was free. It was heart-wrenching to be able to see places I recognized so easily, but in a way, it was also comforting to see that things were still out there and this was not all that was left of the world—as it seemed to me at that time of my life.

After I had been there about six weeks, I decided to get rid of all the useless reading material I had in my cell. If I couldn't learn something from it, out it went. I went to the library and got myself only books I could benefit by reading. Reading was still an escape, but now a little deeper one with a purpose. I began writing poetry that expressed my emptiness. It was all I knew then. Here is one poem I wrote while thinking about someone who was very special to me.

For Ann,
wherever I may find her.

Ann, must I shed tears unto death
in the absence of your loving soul?
Must I toil within without rest,
do I strive for an unreachable goal?

Will my desires be filled with delusions
which are forevermore filling my mind?
Must I be caught in a sea of confusion?
Pray, give sight to the blundering blind.

Winds sweep the darkness and lift the sweet
    fragrance
of the fresh spring fields to my memory's home;
dear, beautiful child whom I met in the spring,
don't you know children should not travel alone?

So wander, my child, into my arms,
wander my way as you roam;
I long to hold you, I love you deeply,
dear, sweet child, I adore you, come home.

Our routine never changed in prison. Bells controlled our lives. The sounds of bells ringing at 6:30 a.m awakened us. At the sound of another bell at 7 a.m., the cell doors would open so we could go to breakfast. After breakfast, we went back to our cells until 8 a.m. Then another bell indicated it was time to go to our job placements. We did the necessary work and then goofed off until 11:30 when we would go back to our cells and get ready for lunch. Bells at noon sent us to lunch. Because the number of inmates allowed in the lunch room at one time was kept to a minimum (in case of a disturbance which could lead to a riot), we ate in shifts. We would go back to our cell until 1 p.m. when another bell meant it was time to go back to work. Work ended at 4:30, with supper at 5:00. The bells marked the day's progress. After supper, we would be locked back up in our cells until it was time for our particular cellblock to go to the gymnasium where we could watch TV, lift weights, or play basketball for 50 minutes. Then it was back to our cells until morning. So, on a weekday, we were confined to our cells for about fourteen hours a day.

> It is not true that "they" cannot lock your heart up, just your body; I still had all the pieces every time "they" locked me up.

On weekends, the routine changed a little. Breakfast was not until 8 a.m. on Saturdays and Sundays. In the winter, we would get our usual 50 minutes in the gymnasium. But, as it warmed up, they would allow us out in the "yard," weather permitting. Sunday there were church services for those who wanted to go. And we would all see a movie in the gym on Sunday afternoon. Then it was back to our cells until Monday morning. So, on weekends, there were some days we spent up to twenty hours a day locked in our cells. If you didn't read or write, it could really get boring.

Here sat 800 inmates doing absolutely nothing that was productive; and when their time was up, they went right back out into the same situation which got them there to begin with. The whole process was ineffective, just like we were.

We could have visitors only on weekends. Although it was nice to have someone to come and visit, it was such a lonely feeling to see them walk through the steel gates to freedom while I was still locked up. My mother came to see me at least every two weeks. At first, I had a girlfriend who would occasionally come to see me, but after a while, except for family members (if you were lucky enough to have any), everyone seemed to forget about you. And when the fellows would go back to their cells after a visit, you could tell they didn't want to talk to anyone. Visits actually brought your mood even further downward. It was easier to deal with the isolation from your friends and family than to see them now and then for an hour or so. At least it seemed that way for me many times. I had a couple of friends who came to see me while I was there, but it was rare. I never had many people I could call friends when I was out there, anyway. Why would I expect a change? My father and one of my brothers came to see me a couple of times, but the whole place was depressing, and people felt it. We would have to sit on opposite sides of a wide table to talk; and when you are surrounded by other people close enough for them to hear your conversation, it is very uncomfortable.

The reformatory housed inmates from the age of 18 to 25. We were the youngest of the adult offenders, quite a bit less mature than our older counterparts. In our immaturity, we created more fights, arguments, and general problems. The only thing we had in common was that we were all young and headed in the wrong direction. Close supervision was necessary to prevent a small problem from escalating into a full-scale riot, which could become a very dangerous situation. Since there were a lot of hotheads in there, there is no question someone could have been seriously hurt.

There were serious penalties for fighting, stealing, harrassing, gambling, etc. And we knew our behavior would, in part, determine how long our stay would be.

They had a place they called "the hole" for inmates who had problems following the rules. This place was in the deepest, darkest part of the prison. No matter how loud an inmate yelled there, none of the rest of the inmate population could hear him. An inmate in the hole was not released from his cell for exercise except very rarely under close supervision, and there were no privileges. He did not receive the same food as the rest of the population; he just got sandwiches and a piece of fruit. He got only the very minimum care—nothing more. A stay in the hole could vary from a couple of days to a month. Then some of the more difficult inmates were simply transferred to "lock-up," which meant they were constantly in their cell except to shower twice a week. If they continued to create problems, they would be transferred to Stillwater State Prison with the older offenders, a place where no one wanted to go. (Besides being a more difficult environment, an inmate's stay there was usually extended as well). The methods of control were effective but primitive, about what you would expect when dealing with immature and confused men.

Those methods did not stop some of the more determined individuals, however. I remember one fellow in particular, on the painting crew, whose job was to maintain the appearance of the buildings. This particular fellow got a ladder that was normally kept under lock and key. He then headed toward the wall with the intention of going over it. He ignored the gun towers until one of the guards yelled and threatened to shoot him. If he had kept going, the guard would have shot him. So this fellow headed back in across the yard to the interior of the prison and made his way to the front gates. There were three gates a person had to pass through to get to freedom. He had a length of pipe about twenty inches long, and he grabbed a guard on his way to the front gate. He told the guard at the first gate if he didn't open it, he was going to beat the guard with the pipe. But the guards are instructed not to open those gates under any circumstances, even if a guard was being threatened. So this fellow began hitting the guard on the head and face with the pipe until the "goon squad" showed up and subdued him.

(The goon squad was the name that the inmates gave to a

particular group of guards whose job it was to go into dangerous situations and resolve them. They were all over six feet tall and looked like wrestlers. They weren't exactly a "friendly" looking bunch. They wore helmets and riot gear, carried clubs and had mace strapped to their belts.)

They took this fellow away to the hole and the guard went to the hospital, since he was pretty badly beaten. No one saw the inmate for a few days, and then, one day, I heard from other inmates that the "goon squad" had escorted him out of the prison. They said that he was covered with bruises and welts. The guards must have worked him over good after they got him in the hole. None of us was surprised, however, since we knew what we could expect if we got out of hand. It was several weeks before the guard who had been beaten returned to work. In the meantime, they transferred the inmate to Stillwater State Prison where he would be doing more time for his attempted escape and assault on a guard. He'd be in there a long time. His offense was one which the parole board would not take lightly.

The sexual situation in the reformatory was not like what you see on television. If someone was involved sexually with another inmate, it was usually by choice. There were some inmates who would perform sexual favors in exchange for money or drugs, but I never heard of anyone being raped while I was there. There were some relationships which were obviously gay. For the most part, they were left alone as long as they didn't bother anyone else. If an inmate was "straight," it was necessary for him to "relive" his memories of sexual encounters. He might have a dream about a girl he had known and wake up and realize where he was. This was reality, and it hurt.

My first Christmas at the reformatory came and went. I don't think it was as bad for me as earlier Christmases I had spent away from home, but, still, it was very lonely and emotionally draining to be locked behind bars when I knew that the rest of my friends and family were enjoying the holidays and the spirit of the Christmas season. In honor of the season, we didn't work Christmas Day and saw a movie, much the same as Sundays. That small treat was our only observance of the occasion. I will never forget looking out those windows beyond my cell and watching the snow falling and drifting, and the way it covered the trees. I thought about happier times when I was home for Christmas with my family and friends.

Holidays are the most difficult times when you are locked up and separated from the people you love. I cannot imagine what those people without families and friends went through. Some inmates never received so much as a letter. For them, there wasn't anything to go back to, except their former hopeless state.

When spring arrived, they would allow us out into the yard to get some exercise or just sit around in the sun. We had to sit in the sun because there were almost no trees anywhere. In the entire reformatory complex, there was only one tree, in an area called the "courtyard," where visits were sometimes allowed if weather permitted. I don't know how it could grow there surrounded by such emptiness, loneliness, and hopelessness. Out in the yard we would gather in groups and just sit around shooting the bull. Occasionally someone would be unselfish enough to share a joint of marijuana with the rest of us, an unusual occurrence because of the high cost of drugs in prison. We could buy three extremely small joints of marijuana for five dollars cash. If an inmate didn't have someone to smuggle cash or drugs to him, the only way to get cash was to buy it using cartons of cigarettes. The exchange rate was about a dollar a carton. Sometimes someone might have a jar of "hooch," homemade liquor they brewed in the rafters of some building for a week or so. It was just sugar, yeast, and fruit left to ferment in a warm place. But I wasn't attracted to alcohol at that time the way I was drawn to other drugs.

There were a few guards walking among us to keep an eye on us, but it was easy enough to keep track of where each one was. The guards in the gun towers would watch us through binoculars, so we had to be aware of them if we were doing anything shady. Most of the time we would just enjoy being out in the fresh air. Aside from clerks and inmates who shoveled snow, there were not many fellows who got outside at all in the winter.

10 If you have become desperate in your search for answers, you are obviously looking in the wrong place.

Y CASEWORKER CALLED ME INTO his office after I had been there about a year. He told me that I had been selected to join a small group of about 24 inmates, chosen because of our attitude and our abilities, who would be allowed to attend college classes inside the reformatory. The instructors were to come from St. Cloud State University. We looked at it as a special opportunity, and it gave us a bit of optimism for a change. We would be attending classes five days a week, and we would be on the same schedule as the rest of the inmates, but, there were some advantages. We would all move to the same cell block with lights which we could control. In all the other cells, lights were controlled by staff and shut off at 10 p.m.

There were a few fellows who gave us a hard time, out of jealousy. But, all in all, most inmates were supportive of the idea. If it worked, there was a plan to enlarge it so others might benefit from it as well. Very few inmates had any special skills, so they viewed this pilot program as a stepping stone, an opportunity that had not existed before. It gave us hope; and if there was one thing everyone in there needed, it was hope.

The name of the college project was Project Newgate. We gathered together as a group and got a run-down of the program from its director and coordinator. They expected us to maintain above-average grades, a goal they felt we should be able to achieve, considering our abilities. The program began to raise our self-esteem immediately. The instructors were all capable and pleasant to work

(Top) Aerial shot of St. Cloud Reformatory; (bottom) interior view.

PHOTOS COURTESY OF STEARNS COUNTY HISTORICAL SOCIETY

with. The fact that we were "cons" didn't seem to bother them. We grew comfortable with one another from the very beginning.

We were an enthusiastic group, there was no question about that. We enjoyed our classes and got away from the prison atmosphere when we were attending "college." Most of us stayed up studying our material very thoroughly so we could do well on the quizzes and tests. Our instructors were surprised at our interest and enthusiasm. It was something they said they didn't see with such intensity in their other students at the University. The average combined grade point average was 3.0 at the end of the first quarter. There were several students who completed the course work with straight A's.

The first two quarters we were limited to general courses. The third quarter we were given a few more choices because of our efforts, and we asked for a drama class. We were cons; and we could act—we had been doing it all our lives. We also requested a course dealing with some of our own problems, a course called Crime and Delinquency. We figured we knew something about that course already. We were looking forward to our third quarter, but first we had to get through another Christmas. That was the end of 1970; I had been locked up for nineteen months.

The mood of the general population lifted after the holidays had passed. You could tell everyone was glad it was behind them. We began our third quarter of college courses. We were glad to be back at it, proud of our achievements and looking forward to new challenges with a growing sense of self respect. We had proved that we had potential; what we lacked most was a sense of direction and a willingness to complete difficult tasks when we were "outside" of prison. We needed momentum, a sense of hope. Hope was in short supply in our group, despite our opportunity to attend the classes and earn college credits. I am very sure that there were some fellows in our group who went on to get their degrees in their chosen field and are very successful in that field. And I am just as sure some of them are happily married with children and have a happy, well-adjusted home life. Unfortunately, I am also very confident some of those guys went on living a life of crime and drugs and ended up dead or in prison.

The most effective class was our theater group. There, we learned how important teamwork was. We performed several plays, which the rest of the inmates greeted with enthusiasm. If you could hold their interest, you knew you were doing a good job. They were a very tough audience. We could even invite members of our family to one of the plays we had performed. And some of the people involved in the theater department as well as a large number of students from St. Cloud State University attended some of our plays, and everyone thought they were very good. We were a convincing group because of our need for—and use of—manipulation and "conning" experiences.

When the class was over and the plays had all been performed, it was difficult to break up the "team." A lot of camaraderie had built up through our experiences together—something that is very rare in a prison setting, something there should be more of.

I completed my third quarter of class work in the spring of 1971. I had acquired about 56 credits with a 3.2 grade point average. I had nothing to do *but* study. It would be a different story when I got out and began attending college with women, drugs, and the ever-present parties that went on in a college town.

I went before the parole board in May of 1971 and was granted parole. My mother and my two youngest brothers came to the reformatory to pick me up. It was spring and everything was so green, completely different from what I had been used to. The air seemed fresher than I could ever remember. It was the smell of freedom.

I spent some time with my mother and brothers, but I didn't stay sitting very long. I ran into my best friend who had visited me in the reformatory. We had done a lot of drugs together. He had some potent marijuana, so we went for a ride in his car and I got very high. I was supposed to be the host of a dinner party my mother was cooking for some theater people I had worked with. By the time my friend dropped me off at my mother's house, not only was I late, but I was very high. I could barely talk without laughing. I'm sure I embarrassed my mother as well as our guests. But they were theater people, so they understood my condition.

Most of them, at the very least, had smoked marijuana.

It turned out to be a nice night; being free was such a treat for me after being locked up for so long. I had ended up serving two years of a twenty-year sentence. So I was on parole when I got out until my parole officer felt I could run my own life. I spent the night with a woman I had met through the theater department, and I never saw her again after that. I got so caught up in the freedom and drugs that I just never went to see her again. This was a perfect example of how selfish I was. I didn't think about how my behavior might affect others. I only cared about satisfying my desires after two years away from life.

I moved into a dormitory at St. Cloud State University, to begin the first summer session there. It was a difficult adjustment for me to make. I felt self-conscious when I was around women. I had a speech class and I was supposed to get up in front of the class and give a speech, but I couldn't bring myself to do it. Performing in a play was different: I was only *part* of the focus. I quit school the first week. It made me uncomfortable, and I had better things to do.

I met a girl who had the same likes (sex and drugs) as I did. We began spending quite a bit of time together. It was the summer of 1971 and the madness of the '60s continued. There was no shortage of drugs. There were more drugs available than when I had been sent to prison two years before. So I spent the summer high on dope and with a number of different women. There was no productivity in my life at all. My relationships were sexual, nothing more.

When I had been out about a month, I went over to pick up some drugs at a dealer's house. No one answered the door, but they had left without locking the door and I walked in. I took all the drugs that were there and a couple of hundred dollars I found stashed away. I was thorough: I knew where to look for hidden dope and money. My mind was working just like the dealers I had been ripping off for years. When that money ran out, I found another place to rob. I hated working, and I would do anything to avoid it, since it interfered with my drug use. I also resented the fact employers paid so little because the work available to me was generally hard work that no one else wanted to do. Yet they would only pay me minimum wage, or close to it. It seemed to me that everyone was still using everyone else, and that nothing had changed, including myself.

I got a nice little apartment near the downtown area. I had no car, so it was handier to be close to the bars and activities after the bars closed. I filled my place with plants and painted it to look real nice. It was quite a change from a six by ten foot cell painted light green with only a toilet, a sink, and a bed. I partied the summer away. I did more than get a taste of freedom, I swallowed it whole. I concentrated on fulfilling my physical desires: dope, women, and drinking. I may have thought I was fulfilling my needs, but my real needs were submerged. I didn't know about love, or trust, or faith, or even hope. I just kept on going and didn't look back at the trail of damage behind me. I was an arrogant know-it-all with an addiction to anything that would take away the pain I felt from living in this world.

My fun ended in early September. I was arrested for possession of marijuana again. I had about one quarter of an ounce.

We have this tendency to be imperfect.

They put me in jail until my parole agent could notify the parole board of my arrest and see what they wanted to do with me. They wouldn't send me back to St. Cloud Reformatory; so if they were going to prosecute me for parole violation, they would have to send me to Stillwater State Prison. Even though the police wanted me locked up, my parole officer decided to give me a break. Marijuana was beginning to be taken less seriously as a crime; there was even a bill in the state legislature to change possession of a small amount of marijuana to a gross misdemeanor.

My father, a lawyer, had helped work out a plan for me to leave the city and get a job. Everyone figured if they couldn't lock me up, they would at least get me out of town. So I headed for Duluth, Minnesota, to work in a meat market for $5 an hour—not exactly the job of my dreams, but at least I wouldn't be in jail or prison. I had no choice. I got out of jail to go home and pack my things.

When I opened my apartment door, I saw that all my beautiful plants were dead. I had forgotten about them while I was in jail for those couple of weeks. In a way it was a good representation of how my life was going. I felt dead, lifeless, and hopelessly lost in what seemed to be a never-ending cycle of one disappointment and loss after another.

I arrived in Duluth with everything I owned in a couple of bags. I found a cheap hotel near the place where I was going to be working and got settled in. It was a little light green room with a single window, a toilet, a bed, and a sink. It reminded me of days gone by. The only thing missing were the bars.

The job was not too bad, but it was impossible to save enough money for me to get cheerier living quarters. The whole situation depressed the hell out of me! I was alone, knew no one, and just drank myself to sleep each night. There was a Christmas party, and I got in a fight with the meat-market owner's grandson. That gave me a good excuse to quit my job. I didn't know what I was going to do, but I knew I didn't want to grind up dead animals the rest of my life.

i would rather wash the sea
          with stones and pebbled seaweed
          than to shelter storms
          raging
          ravaging their way homeward

if i had not my sea-saw world of treasures
          to grace my sandy hillside
          all year round
          i would leave the seas unto
          themselves
and travel through a teacup world
     on a small dish of pewter
          only to eventually

                              break
                              falling
                              from
                              some
                              withered

                    sailor's
                    hand . . .

                         —*Written in prison, Spring, 1971*

11

We sometimes allow our children to make mistakes, that they might learn. So does our Father in heaven.

GOT IN TOUCH WITH A FRIEND THAT I knew from reform school and my forestry camp days. He used dope and drank too, so at least I wasn't completely alone. He had a good job working on the ships that came into Duluth. He made just enough to support his wife and their new child. He couldn't get me a job with him, but we spent his time off drinking and using whatever drugs we could get our hands on. But I was running out of the little bit of money I had left from my final check, so I was getting worried. I was so depressed that I went to the Mental Health Center to see if I could talk to anyone that might be able to help me feel better about myself.

They sent me to see a psychiatrist who was an advisor on the board of directors for a children's home. He thought my experience might be valuable in working with delinquent teens, and he arranged an interview with the children's home for me that day. They hired me to start work as a night watchman the next evening. I was excited. The wage was a little better than I had been used to, and my job was certainly easy enough.

There wasn't much training involved. I spent the first night with another watchman who explained how things worked. I started the second night working by myself. The home had both boys and girls from the ages of about ten through seventeen. They slept and lived on separate floors of the home. My primary purpose was to keep them apart during the night. They were sneaky, but I was sneakier so I usually caught them if they tried to meet after lights out. I got along real well with the kids. We could relate to one another because of the similarities of our lives.

It was the first job that I really liked and felt competent in performing. There was an opening for another person on the day shift, so they offered me the position and I jumped at it. My job was to supervise the kids and to help them stay involved in productive activities. We participated in sports with the kids, played pool or cards, or went on outings to the movies or a park, etc. When summer came, I took them on trips into the Boundary Waters Canoe Area. I thought it was the best job in the world. I got paid to take these kids camping and fishing! We had some really good trips.

They picked me to work with two of the most difficult boys because the rest of the staff thought I could relate to them. We would go hiking around the forests in the Duluth area. I took them camping and fishing and taught them about the woods. They learned how to set up camp and keep things organized. We spent a lot of time fishing. They were tough kids to communicate with, but when you were able to get through to them, it made all the effort worth it.

Some years later, one of the boys I had taken out on these trips ran away from the children's home in the middle of winter. They found him dead of exposure inside someone's hunting cabin in the north woods of Duluth. I felt really bad for this kid. I knew he loved the freedom of the woods and of the outdoors, and that's all he was looking for. I could relate to his search very easily.

I worked at the children's home for about a year. We were at a summer camp for two weeks when they suspected me of smoking pot. I denied it, but they felt they had enough evidence to terminate my employment. During this year, my drinking had reached new heights. I was buying liquor every day after work and then going home to drink until I would fall asleep. I thought it helped to lessen the effects of my loneliness.

My search for a new job proved fruitless. I was an ex-con, and I had just been fired from my job—not much in the way of references. I began using drugs and alcohol much more frequently. I started in the morning and continued until I passed out or fell asleep. Then I ran into a woman I knew who was looking for a pound of pot to buy. She offered me some money if I could help her. I needed the money, so we headed to St. Cloud where I knew I could get her all the dope she wanted.

We got to St. Cloud about nine o'clock that night. It didn't take long to locate what we were looking for. I ran into someone who knew somebody else who had about twelve or fourteen pounds of marijuana. It just so happened, this fellow walked into the bar we were at about five minutes later. I talked to him and he invited me to go out to his car and smoke some to see if I liked it.

It turned out this fellow had all the marijuana with him in the back seat of his rental car. It was too tempting of an opportunity to just let it pass; so after we had gone back inside, I told him I wanted to think about it for a little while, then I slipped back out the door of the bar and broke into his car. I got a duffel bag full of marijuana and transferred it to the trunk of my car. I went back in to get the person who had come with me.

We were just getting into my car when a crowd gathered. The guy got suspicious of my urgency to leave and he checked his car. When he found his pot missing, he knew who had taken it. A crowd of people began to surround my car and weren't going to let me leave. I was carrying a gun, and I just jumped out of the car and fired a shot in the air so everyone would know I meant business. They backed off, and I drove away.

"Bold" was not the word for what I had just done in the middle of a city—"stupid" was a much more appropriate word.

I took an alternate route to Duluth. I felt sure, that this fellow would alert the police and highway patrol. So I went well out of my way to come into Duluth by a different route than the one a person would normally take.

I found out later my hunch was right. The fellow had called the police and the highway patrol with a description of my car.

I sold one of the pounds of pot to the person who had come with me, and planned to sell the rest as I needed the money.

I figured I had come out pretty good. If anyone intended

to take this pot away from me, they had better come with guns; it was mine now. The way I was thinking was far from healthy.

In a few days, the Duluth police approached me. They said they were checking on a report that I had a lot of marijuana in my possession from a drug rip-off in St. Cloud. When they said that, they were almost sitting on the spot I had hidden the pot! I told them they had bad information.

I had worked as an investigator for my father's law firm on several different occasions, and somehow they were aware of that. They knew quite a bit of my background; obviously they had checked up on me. They suggested I work for them. I asked what was in it for me, and they said they could pay me well if my information was helpful. I was really strung out on cocaine at this time, and I knew I would be out of money soon, so I told them I'd see if I could help them. What did I care? No one gave a damn about me. Why should I worry about anyone else? To me this line of thought made perfect sense. I would just play both ends against the middle. I wasn't concerned with anyone but myself.

I set up a few people for selling dope, but I was careful not to expose *my* connections. With the money the police gave me, I bought dope and continued to shoot it into my arms. The police knew about my addiction, but they didn't care as long as I was producing arrests for them. Then they cheated me out of some money I felt I had coming, so I told them it was all over.

It just so happened there was an agent from the Minnesota Bureau of Criminal Apprehension in the room where the conversation took place. He knew my connections with drug dealers, so he offered me more money and told me he would treat me a lot better than the Duluth police would. I told him I would give it a try.

Since I knew a lot of people from the St. Cloud area, they suggested we start there. So I began to introduce agents into the groups of people dealing dope. No one suspected me at first, but things began to change as the agents made more and more "controlled buys," the term for undercover purchases from the dealers. After about six months, they made their arrests: sixteen people for selling drugs to undercover narcotics agents.

It was no secret I had helped in those arrests and my reputation took a turn for the worse. No one trusted me now, neither the law nor the dealers. It was not a comfortable feeling. I just told myself I didn't care that I wouldn't have any friends left after this chapter in my life. But in my heart, I knew what I had done. Money and dope spoke louder than loyalty. This situation is not unusual in the drug world.

> # Sorrow is a dead and dry desert stretching for endless distances in our hearts.

I might have picked up the pieces of my life had there been any pieces left. I was now an outcast from the criminal element, as well as from society. There were rumors of "contracts" out on my life. I just bought a bigger gun and kept alert.

From St. Cloud, I moved on to other towns, supporting my drug habit with the money the Bureau of Criminal Apprehension paid me. They would send me into a town, show me pictures of the suspected dealers, and tell me where they hung out. From there it was easy to go into a bar and shoot pool with people and just mingle until I found what I was looking for. No one had any reason not to trust me in these new towns. I bought their dope and they saw me shooting it into my veins. It was easy, and it was adventurous. It filled my need for excitement. What more could I ask for? I would introduce the agents to the necessary people, and then move on to another city.

I had some extra money, so I decided to go somewhere quiet and take a break. I went down to Iowa. After I had spent most of the money I had, I contacted the Organized Crime Unit in Iowa looking for work. They checked with other agencies I had worked for and agreed to put me to work. They sent me to the Quad Cities (where Iowa and Illinois meet), a rough area. It went exactly as it had been in Minnesota, except I could tell I was dealing with a much more dangerous group of people. A lot of the dealers carried guns and were involved in a lot more than just dope. I had to be on my toes. There were some tense situations when people got suspicious, but I always managed to cover my tracks. As things went on, I became much more aware of the ever-present danger.

Some-times, it can really get lonely in a place called "self."

I went home to St. Cloud to take a break, not sure I wanted to continue working undercover. Unfortunately, the damage was done. I had no friends who felt they could trust me. If I felt lonely before, now I really felt alone. I had alienated everyone. My life was in shambles more than ever before. I was destroying everything in my path. I began to drink more heavily than before, counting on the alcohol to help me get through the day if I could not locate or afford the drugs I was craving.

I changed my name legally in 1973, switching my middle name with my last name. I was tired of people asking my name, then saying, "Oh, I've heard about you!" Unfortunately, my name was the only thing changed—not my attitude.

It was shortly after this time I met the woman who later became my second wife. She was 15 years old just turning 16 when we met. I was 25 years old. Our age difference did not go over well with her mother who she lived with, or with her grandfather who had been the assistant chief of police in St. Cloud and knew me well. He had participated in several of my arrests. He was very familiar with my history. But since his granddaughter had just turned 16 years old, there was nothing they could do to stop our relationship, 16 being the age of consent in the State of Minnesota.

She and I spent most of our time together. We went fishing

and camping a lot, not just because of our love for outdoor activities, but also because we had no money for rent or food most of the time. I had stopped shooting drugs shortly before I met her, and I was relying on the alcohol to make my life bearable. I still had a very difficult time finding work, and even if I was able to find a job, I lost it because of my drinking and my attitude. Employers didn't consider me reliable. I was extremely irresponsible and self-centered; and these things, coupled with my addictions, left little room for any positive growth.

I robbed a place and I knew I would have to leave the state to get rid of the merchandise. It was traceable and I didn't need any more problems. I left for warmer climates, leaving my girlfriend behind. I went to Florida for a few months, sold what I had, and ended up spending the money on dope and liquor. I missed my girlfriend, so I decided to head back to Minnesota to be with her again. We picked up where we had left off. It was nice to be back with her, but it was obvious no one else wanted anything to do with me. So we started traveling, seeking our fortune, so to speak. I didn't realize that what I needed and wanted so badly was inside myself, not in another city or state.

We decided to head into northern Minnesota to look for work in a resort. It was early spring and still very cold, but we knew we would be the first to apply for many jobs and that would give us an advantage. We ended up in the coldest spot in the nation— International Falls. We arrived just in time for a big blizzard forecast on the weather reports. We got a newspaper and made a couple of calls. There were not a lot of jobs listed yet. We did manage to set up an interview with a couple who were looking for some caretakers for a private resort. But that interview was not scheduled until

> Evil ultimately destroys itself, just as a flower will die without water. Where there is no love—there is no life.

the next day, and we didn't have enough money to spend on a motel. I felt I needed what we had for liquor. So we ended up sleeping in our car. It was well below zero that night, but if we got cold, we just ran the car for some heat and bundled up tighter in our blankets. We were used to "making do."

The couple who interviewed us were surprised to learn we had slept in our car the night before. They were convinced we were determined people, and, consequently, we got the job. We would live on an island on the Rainy River. There was a private resort on this island owned by a corporation out of Minneapolis. We were to make sure everything was operating properly and if it wasn't, we were to fix it. People came to stay in the summer, but their visits were infrequent.

We had a little one-bedroom cabin overlooking the river. It was nice after we cleaned it up and fixed a few things that had been ignored for some time. It was a good setup. In the summer we would use the corporate boats to take people back and forth between the mainland and the island. In the winter we would use snowmobiles to go in to get groceries. We received a salary and the cabin rent free. I thought I had died and had gone to heaven.

Things went well for the first few weeks, but then my girlfriend started to get cabin fever. She missed her mother who was living in Florida by this time. She called her mother and planned a short visit. She was going to fly down to Florida, and then come back in about a week or so. Two days after she left, I got a letter from her stating that she was sorry, but she could not live on that island and she was going to stay in Florida with her mother. I lasted another four or five days and then quit, and headed to Florida to find her.

I arrived in Florida about a week later. All I had to go on to locate Nancy was the postmark on the letter she had sent me— Jacksonville, Florida. That's where I started looking. I knew Nancy would be on the beach, so I began checking out all the beaches in and around Jacksonville. After about a week, I was running out of money. I was still drinking heavily and smoking pot, and those were expensive habits. I was planning on giving up the search and heading back to Minnesota, but I made one last effort to get the phone number of Nancy's mother. I began calling information for the larger surrounding cities. I got lucky and located her in Daytona Beach.

I called, and Nancy was surprised to hear from me. She told me her new address, and I headed in that direction. She welcomed me with open arms. Her enthusiasm made me feel relieved. I was afraid she had lost interest in me and I would be alone in a strange city. The "aloneness" scared me the most.

The only job I could find because of my limited skills was cutting the lawns of some of the wealthier people. It was discouraging to see those beautiful homes and know how far I was away from having someplace to call home. I had rented a room, but it wasn't any place I wanted to call home for very long. Working all day in the hot sun and drinking all evening after work turned out to be a drain on my system. I was not used to the heat. I was beet red every day after work. And liquor did not replace the liquids I lost while sweating in Florida's hot sunshine. I felt like I had a sunstroke all the time. They paid me five dollars an hour. It was like being trapped in hell.

Eventually, I talked Nancy into going back to Minnesota—no easy task. But it was summer which made it a little easier, since we would not be going back to snow and freezing temperatures. 🕊

12 Despair is the opposite of God.

E SPENT THE SUMMER OF 1975 IN Minnesota, camping on the shores of the Mississippi River. It was better than paying rent. I continued using underhanded tactics to get the money I needed to buy liquor and dope. I seldom worked if I could help it. I know I would have had an easier time getting a job and keeping it if I could have made enough money to live on, but we never seemed to have enough money whether I was working or not.

As fall got closer, carrying with it the threat of winter, we decided to head for Denver, Colorado. I had been there for a while a few years before in my wanderings and I thought it would be a nice place for us to move to. I was hoping for a new beginning.

We arrived in Denver with very little money, so we had to work fast to get on our feet. We saw an ad in the paper for a couple to manage an apartment house. We applied for the job, making up the work history that we would need for this job. We got the job and moved into our new apartment the next day. The rent was included in our salary arrangement, and the owner said we could give her a little each week towards a damage deposit. It was a fast solution to many of our problems.

We made just barely enough to get by on. My drinking and my use of pot and cigarettes cost me about $400 a month. It was no wonder we were always broke.

The building was in a rough neighborhood surrounded by bars. We had some tenants who had simply refused to pay rent for months. Most of them said they just didn't have the money. I cracked down on them with the help of the owner and the police and courts. But even after most of them left, we seemed to get the same type of people looking for apartments. They would pay their first month's rent and then just wait to be evicted. They knew that process would take at least a month, usually more. But I have to admit, it was a good learning experience. It reinforced my feelings of contempt for people in general: they lied, they stole, they couldn't be trusted or depended on, and were basically a bunch of deadbeats. I was becoming more and more hostile toward people, believing my feelings were justified—while, in truth, I was no better than the worst of those I dealt with.

Nancy and I decided to get married in Denver. Her mother and my father flew into Denver to attend the wedding. We also invited a couple of our friends from Minnesota to come out for it. We got married in our apartment and then spent a couple of days in a motel in the mountains. We made plans to leave Denver and just drive northwest into the mountains until we found a place we thought we would like to live. We had been in the center of a big city too long and we both wanted a change. We packed the car and headed out, hoping things would improve for us.

We drove until we got to a little town in Idaho. We rented a motel room and went out to get a newspaper to see if there were any jobs available in the area. There wasn't much, but we found an ad for a home for rent out in the country. We called the number that evening and set up an appointment to see the home the next day. The rent was $160 a month, and we thought we could afford that. When we saw the house, we rented it right away. It wasn't furnished, but we weren't worried about that. We could get by; we always had. From our living room window, we could look out and see a snowcapped mountain. It was beautiful; it didn't matter that we didn't have a chair to sit in. We figured furnishings would come later.

I got a job as a salesman in a hardware store in a town not too far away from our home. It was about a 12-mile drive. The job was boring, but it was all that was available in this small town. I began building picnic tables and porch swings to sell because we sure couldn't live on what I brought home from the hardware store, since my addictions were eating up so much money each month.

Nancy stayed home, and she got pretty bored after about six weeks of this. She talked about going to see her mother. I knew from past experience how strong that pull was. I got her to be patient a little longer, but I could understand her restlessness. We had been there about two months when we just picked up and left. We didn't tell anyone—not our landlord, not my place of work, not even the couple of friends we had made during our short stay. We had a few pieces of used furniture we had bought. We left those things, too. We just disappeared. I'm sure people wondered what had happened to us, but we didn't give it a thought. We were on the road again.

This time we headed to Minnesota to visit with my family and then down to Florida to see Nancy's mother. It felt good to be traveling again. There was nothing I regretted leaving behind. I was hoping somehow our situation would improve. It seemed like things could only get better.

We arrived in Minnesota in late summer. We stayed long enough to get organized and get a little money together for the trip to Florida. Nancy's mother was expecting us in Florida, so at least we had a place to stay until we could get work. My relationship with Nancy's mother had improved somewhat over the years, but there was still a lot of resentment left over from earlier times. We put up with each other—that was about the extent of it. I was an alcoholic and a drug user; she was a nurse in a treatment center. It wasn't hard to see why she didn't care for me very much. I was not the easiest person in the world to deal with; I had all the answers, at least I thought I did. It never occurred to me I might be wrong about something. I could not take criticism well, even if it was justified, an attitude I remember being strong in my father.

When we arrived in Florida, we stayed with Nancy's mother for a few days. We found a job managing a small dilapidated motel on the main street of Daytona Beach. The owner had a lot of money; he was also an alcoholic. As time went by, he would accuse us of renting out rooms and not giving him the money. The motel was so small that it was impossible to embezzle money. The few rooms we had for rent were located in the front of the motel in plain view. The fellow would get paranoid and irrational sometimes, and it got more and more difficult to work for him.

> My drinking and my drug use were merely symptoms of my way of thinking; my fear and my confusion deeply affected my attitude.

Then Nancy discovered she was pregnant with our child. That turn of events gave us the extra little push we needed to plan a move. We decided to go back to Minnesota and try to get ourselves into a situation where we could settle down as a family— although, by this time, my drinking had increased and there were many problems between Nancy and me.

I started a wood-working shop with money my father had loaned me. It got us by for a while, but our financial situation was always critical. My habits were draining our resources as fast as they came in. With the baby due in the middle of the coming summer, my father offered us a job managing a motel he owned. It was a good opportunity and probably could have developed into something worthwhile had it not been for my drinking. I had no enthusiasm, no initiative, absolutely no zest for life. I was just hanging on. The effects of the alcohol were stifling all possibility of growth. I got up, ate something, and would start drinking about two in the afternoon. I'd just sit around drinking and doing nothing. I had no sense of direction or motivation. Whether I drank or not, I was not happy. I was trapped inside of what I had become and I could not get out.

The day our son was born I was camping in northern Minnesota, so it was quite a surprise to arrive home the next day and discover I was a father. It was exciting to have a new addition to our family. It seemed so different. But this change was permanent, and I knew in my heart I was not prepared emotionally to handle this responsibility. With the birth of my son, John, my involvement in criminal activities diminished. I wanted to become a better person and give my son a promising future. But my drug and alcohol abuse continued and canceled out any strides I made forward. I hadn't even matured enough to care for myself, let alone a family.

After a couple of months, the difficulties between Nancy and me escalated. My drinking was always an issue, but I wouldn't admit it. I blamed my problems on everyone else. There were a few incidents when the police were called because of our fights. They would take Nancy and our son to a women's shelter. I was certainly emotionally abusive with Nancy, but I never hit her or my son. I felt that my wife often pushed me to my limits intentionally, enabling her to "get even." I don't see anything surprising about her behaving in that way; I was a selfish, arrogant drunkard. In my guilt, I probably felt I had deserved the consequences I suffered. I wasn't much of a husband or a father. I contributed only minimally to the needs of my family.

She left me and took our son, John, to Florida with her. She stayed with her mother for a couple of weeks and eventually came back. It became a pattern. It happened several times during the period when we managed the motel. I think we were both very unhappy, but we didn't know how to change.

Eventually, I reached a point where I had destroyed any trust my father had for me. He discovered I had rented rooms and never given him payment. I had threatened one motel guest with a shotgun. The police had to be called on a number of occasions, and he just got tired of all the lies and trouble. He told us we had thirty days to find somewhere else to work and live.

There was no denying it. I had taken advantage of every situation I could. I could not be trusted. I demonstrated no responsibility. I was lazy and didn't complete jobs I was supposed to take care of. It was hard to blame my father. I had left him no choice.

We moved to the Twin Cities area and found a job as assistant managers of a fairly large apartment complex. I managed to complete my assigned jobs well enough to keep the job, but I was still able to spend a great deal of the day drinking. Again we never had enough money because of the expense of my habits. I was drinking a lot of beer every day, smoking pot, and two packs of cigarettes. With the cost of these habits, it was no wonder we didn't have enough money to survive. It required one-third of our income to support my addictions.

We kept that job for about a year before I got fed up with doing all the work that had to be done at the complex. The manager would just give me a list of jobs to do each day and then disappear. He was supposed to be working with me. It had started out that way, but things had changed after we had been there a couple of months. I was getting bored anyway, and looked forward to a change.

We located a job managing 150 luxury apartments in St. Paul, Minnesota. The people we worked for were impressed with my knowledge of building maintenance and Nancy's ability to work well with people. It didn't hurt that Nancy was extremely attractive. They hired us for the job and we moved into our new apartment the following week. We were the managers of this complex, and we had two sets of caretakers to help us keep it operating at an acceptable level. Nancy stayed at home, taking phone calls and showing the apartments when we had a vacancy. I handled the maintenance of the buildings and delegated the responsibilities to our caretakers. In the beginning I did my share of work, but as time passed, I took advantage of the situation and eventually I was delegating all the responsibilities of the job to our caretakers. It was easy to do after I had been there awhile. The buildings were in good shape, so we didn't have any major repairs. I was there if I was needed, sitting in our

Hell is a place that we hollow out of our loneliness to crawl further into ourselves.

apartment drinking.

Nancy's pattern of going to Florida when we had problems continued. After a week or two of her getting down there, I was able to talk her into coming back. But those plane fares were not cheap, so this expense added to our existing problems.

> I have been inside of myself so long, there are no new places to hide, so the hurt always finds me—only now with more intensity and frequency.

We lasted almost a year at that job. Nancy finally took John and went to Florida to live with her mother. This time she wasn't coming back like the other times. I lost the job because we had been hired as a couple and with Nancy gone, the company didn't think I could handle the job myself. I packed what I would need for my trip to Florida and sold the rest of the things we had acquired over the past year. Once again I went after Nancy. Even if she wanted to leave me, I did not think she had the right to separate me from our son by taking him so far away. I left Minnesota with the intention of getting back together or at the very least, bringing John back to Minnesota.

By the time I arrived in Florida, Nancy had a boyfriend. His name was John as well, so he was "Big John" and my son, "Little John." It was just as though my son had been taken away from me. I spent about three weeks down in Florida trying to convince Nancy to come back and try it again—much of those three weeks in a room I rented drinking and crying. I was closer to attempting suicide than I had ever been. If I had had a gun, I'm almost sure I would have followed through with it. I felt so alone and everything looked so hopeless. I didn't feel I had any reason to go on living. It was the lowest I had ever felt and the use of alcohol only depressed me further.

I made arrangements to pick John up for a day. I was packed and ready to take him back to Minnesota. I called Nancy that afternoon when we were well out of Florida and told her I was taking our son back home where he belonged. I kept the conversation short because I knew Nancy had the habit of getting pretty excited, and I didn't want her to get hysterical. I told her I would be in touch with her once I got settled.

Once we have wandered from our path, our life becomes a search, and we have left the truth behind.

I stopped to see my mother when we got back to St. Cloud, but I didn't stay long. I knew Nancy would create some problems if she could. I headed into northern Minnesota where I had a few friends. I knew I had to come up with a plan. I was not used to caring for John all day. I hadn't realized how busy a 2 year old boy could be.

A friend of mine in the area where I was living with John told me she was interested in selling her daycare center to me. She had owned it for six or seven years and was getting bored with it and wanted to do something else. She had a rental agreement for a house to be used for a daycare center. It was licensed for 24 children, but she only had about six kids there then, so it wasn't bringing in much money. I recognized its potential and made arrangements to take it over. She would accept monthly payments, with no money down. I felt that I couldn't lose. Not only that, but I realized I was solving two problems at once: I now had a job and a place for John to be while I worked, with me. It seemed perfect.

I went back to St. Cloud to pick up some belongings I had left at my mother's house. The phone rang, and it was my wife. She had arrived in St. Cloud, and she told me she wanted to get back together and try it again. I thought her offer was too good to be true. I told her I had bought a daycare center somewhere up north. I thought having her there was great because Nancy could help me run the daycare center, and we would still be with our son. My spirits were lifted; I saw some hope. I told her to come over to my mother's apartment and we would leave from there. She showed up about half an hour later. She seemed sullen and withdrawn, but I attributed it to our separation. We got everything packed and headed out the door.

As we were approaching the car, two very large deputy sheriffs took John from me and gave him to my wife. They informed me that Nancy had made a statement to the authorities claiming I was abusive and there was reason to believe our son's welfare was in jeopardy. She said she was afraid I would hurt our son if they tried to take him from me. I found out later that the deputies had followed me for two days looking for an opportunity to get my son safely.

The whole idea was ludicrous. I would never had done anything to hurt my son, ever. I was hurt terribly by the lies, and hurt further because others believed those lies.

I tried to get on with my life. Nancy and I were divorced, and the court gave Nancy custody of our son, along with permission to move to Florida.

13 There is no way to sin discreetly.

OLLOWING THROUGH ON MY PLAN, I purchased the daycare center. Through advertising and word of mouth, I reached our licensing capacity of 24 children. I placed our emphasis on learning, not just playing. We were now a pre-school, not simply a daycare center. I built it up so that I could afford to have someone responsible to run the center so I didn't have to worry about it. That arrangement left me free to do my drinking. I was very careful never to have any contact with the parents of the children if I had alcohol on my breath. I lived in the basement of the house I rented for my center, so I was still able to keep tabs on everyone with the help of an intercom system.

Regardless of my addiction to alcohol, I ran a tight ship. I took the responsibility of those children very seriously. I made sure the situation was in good hands before I'd disappear about two or three in the afternoon to begin my drinking. In the beginning, I stayed around a lot to make sure everything would run smoothly, but as my confidence grew with my staff, I started going to the bars in town in mid-afternoon.

Things were going better than I could have ever hoped. There was plenty of money coming in. I was meeting the needs of the children, and I began to feel I had some value after all. My business was helping my self-esteem and self-confidence. I finally felt that I was contributing something worthwhile. I was fast becoming successful, a feeling I was unfamiliar with. Unfortunately, my drinking began to escalate. I would go to restaurants for lunch and end up staying there through happy hour. Then I would pick up a twelve-pack of beer to take home to continue my drinking, wake up and do it again.

My relationships were just as superficial as they had been previously in my life. I had difficulty getting close to people. Merely being successful in business had not helped to solve any of my very real problems—just the opposite. I believed it created more problems for me. I now had the money I needed to pursue my addictions without doing anything criminal. I considered it a blessing initially; but as time went by, I found myself further and further from the peace, contentment, and satisfaction that I had expected to accompany feelings of success. I was beginning to realize I was losing control, but in my arrogance, I refused to admit it or take any steps to correct the problem.

> If we could see our attitude when we looked in a mirror, we would either stop looking—or make some serious changes.

After a financially successful year, I wanted to enlarge the operation to meet the needs of the community. I started looking for a building to rent or buy that would allow me to care for more children. I found a building that I thought would be ideal, and after several letters and conversations with my father, he agreed to help me finance the building. He was aware of my drinking problem, but I don't think he knew the degree to which I needed alcohol to cope with this world. Furthermore, he was hoping for my success. He was as tired of my failures as I was.

With the help of some friends, we gutted the inside of the

building and started to build a pre-school that would provide the best opportunities for the children. In addition to living quarters for myself, the building had two bathrooms, three classrooms, a very large room for a play area, and a kitchen. We covered the floor with colorful carpet squares and painted all the rooms. I found a deal on four computers and purchased four 19-inch televisions for monitors. We put these computers in a special area where we had constructed partitions so the children could work on them without distractions. The rooms were filled with plants and brightly colored pictures. It was beautiful when we got done. I was very proud of what we had created; it was truly a place for children to learn and grow.

We were licensed by the State of Minnesota to care for up to 44 children. We were full within thirty days.

A friend that I had known since my early teen years came to work for me. He was especially skilled in the area of diplomacy, which was important when we were dealing with people's dearest possession, their children. When tested by the State for his child development skills, he scored the highest of anyone ever evaluated by that particular examiner. His skills were exceptional. But he had one problem: he, too, was an alcoholic like myself. He maintained his sobriety quite well. He had a couple of slip-ups, but managed to get back on his feet each time. He was invaluable in running the operation. I trusted him implicitly. This set-up allowed me to continue drinking and wasting money just as fast as it came in. If there was one thing I was good at, it was delegating responsibility to others so I would end up able to do exactly as I wanted.

Nancy got in touch with me and wanted to get back together, but I was not sure that arrangement was what I wanted by that time. I was dating a number of women who brought their children to my preschool. She came up and brought John with her. At first it went real well, but it went right back to the way it had been before. I was an alcoholic; it was very difficult to fulfill the role of husband and father with that anchor around my neck. I was sick of it, but it had me in its grip and I honestly felt I would be a drunk forever. When my priority was "getting high," I had little room for family life.

I remember praying for the removal of my addiction to alcohol. It was the summer of 1983. I had been seriously addicted to alcohol and other drugs for nineteen years. I had no trouble seeing the debris I left behind me, which was, in fact, little pieces of my life. It was crumbling more and more each day. I hated it, but I had no control over it.

I decided I would go through treatment for alcoholism. I just couldn't deal with my losses anymore. I expected them to cure me, but I found out it didn't work that way. There was no way I could be fixed externally. It had to happen internally but I didn't realize it at the time. Although I put a lot of effort into my treatment, I was back drinking the day after I was released. My hopes fell lower with my failure. I just could not resist drinking. It seemed the only refuge from my pain—the pain I could not talk to anyone about. Because I trusted no one, I knew even if I did find people I could talk to, they could never understand where I was unless they also had been there. I felt sure most people had not been where I had been; and, therefore, could not understand my feelings. I hid from everything that could touch me deeply. I was tired of being hurt. I was tired of living. I was clinging to hope, of which I had little.

The reality of earth imitates hell.

In 1984 I began to gamble. I learned the only thing worse than a drunk was a drunk-who-gambled. I started out well enough; it seemed I was winning pretty consistently for the first few months. Then came a night I lost $500. It was all downhill from there. I would go out with the intention of not gambling; but after I got enough liquor in me, out would come my money, or worse yet, my checkbook. I had been around long enough and been successful enough that I had no problems cashing large checks at the bars and restaurants I frequented. I had running tabs in most of them. Gambling was a habit a lot like drinking: you start out with hope and the best of intentions, and end up being helplessly sucked into it. I never went anywhere without gambling. It became like the drink in my hand, a part of me. I actually had dreams about winning a lot of money. I was obsessed with getting something for nothing, much as I had been most of my life.

By now, Nancy and John had left for good. They were living in Florida. She, too, felt the lack of hope. She may have envisioned something I had not been able to see, the finality of the situation I was in. I was spinning downward into a hole; it was only a matter of time before I hit the bottom.

I got behind on my taxes first, since they were the easiest thing to put off. Then I got behind on some bills for work that had been done for me by some businesses in town. In looking back now, I can remember the utter hopelessness I was filled with. I dreaded each day until I got high and drunk, then I was safe again. I didn't worry or care about anything.

My gambling became more intense. I had fallen so far behind, that I was hoping to catch up. The more depressed I got, the more I drank; the more I drank, the more I gambled; the more I gambled, the more I lost, which only depressed me further. It was a vicious cycle, and I could not stop it. I began to lose larger amounts of money. One night I lost $700; I went home and cried. I had an accountant do my books and found out I was $15,000 behind. I had ignored my bills and my taxes as well as a lot of bills to bars and restaurants. I was in over my head and I knew it. My life had become so internally miserable; I just didn't care about anything at all anymore. I just gave up. I made plans to close the pre-school at the end of 1984. I just wanted out, but I had absolutely no idea what I would do. I didn't care.

I had a sale and sold everything in the place. I can recall how the place looked after everything was gone, so empty, much like my dreams.

I continued living in the building after I shut down the business. I just drank all day, from waking up until I passed out, only to wake up and do it again. All the people with whom I had established friendships through the years in my business were gone. They knew what I had become. Despair became a world I had to live in. This big, empty, lonely building filled with only memories of what used to be, seemed an appropriate setting. I felt the way it looked. Where once it had been a harbor, it was now an island.

I began frequenting some of the rougher bars in town, pools halls and places where drugs were used by almost everyone in the place—my kind of place, where a desperate person would fit in—somewhere *I* would fit in. I kept to myself most of the time. I didn't have anything to say to anyone. I don't even know why I went to those places. Maybe I just hoped to escape the loneliness I held within myself.

Every day was a battle. I'd get up and start drinking right away, and then I'd sit and look at where the computer terminals were torn out of the wall, so I could sell the plywood to get money for booze. I'd look at the only plants I had left. They were all dead. Beer and liquor bottles were lying all over. Cigarette butts were piled high in some can I found to use for an ashtray. Outside the playground was empty of children; gone too were the swing sets, teeter totter, and slides—all sold so I could pay for my drug use and gambling. I even sold my bed and all my furniture. I slept in a corner on a cot, and covered myself with the only nice thing I had left, a big, soft, beautiful quilt, which someone broke in and stole while I was getting drunk at some bar one night. It was the only thing I had worth taking.

Winter passed and my father told me I'd have to find somewhere else to stay. He was putting the building up for sale. He didn't need to say it, but I knew he didn't need a drunk around there. It wouldn't help the appearance of the building. So, I packed what I had into a bag, got in my car (which was on the verge of being repossessed,) and drove off. I found a job caretaking some lake property in exchange for the rent on a little tiny cabin. My job was to cut the lawn of the home and help with odd jobs occasionally. I was out of money except for what I could beg, borrow, or steal. In my exasperation, I applied for welfare assistance. I was approved to receive $203 at the beginning of each month, and about $100 in food stamps each month. I spent it all on liquor; it was more important than food. I would usually find someone to buy my food stamps, which would give me a little more cash, but always for about half of what they were worth.

> # I had become a participant of sorrow in an endless downward plunge.

In one of my lower moments in this cabin, I decided to put an end to all of this. There was no value in my life at all. I felt I had sunk as low as a person could go. My existence was not only useless, but tormented; I wanted to die. I went out to find a hose to put over my exhaust pipe and run into the car; but when I went looking for my car keys, I couldn't find them. I was really hopeless. I looked everywhere, but I could not find those keys. When I got up the next morning, they were lying right on the night table at the side of my bed. I thought I was really going nuts.

My instinct for survival had kept thoughts like suicide at bay for many years, although I know there was not a year in my life when it was not a consideration after I had turned 12 years old.

There were those who thought I was just having a great time using drugs and drinking. They could not comprehend the fact that I was doing those things out of desperation. I didn't like the way I felt when I wasn't high; I didn't care much for reality. Earth did not seem like a very good place to be. I was afraid, and I was hiding: it was as simple as that. I was filled with frustration, pain, and resentment. Where was the love, the kindness, the patience, the hope for tomorrow? Where were all those things I'd heard about as a child? Where was the truth I set out to find?

I continued to hang out in bars in that town for about another three months. By then I had reached such a low that I decided I had to try going through treatment for alcoholism again. This time I would go to St. Cloud Hospital; at least I would be close to some of my family.

I was in treatment for about 35 days that time. I felt there might be some hope for me after all. But I was only out three days before I started using alcohol and drugs again. This was in 1986. My future certainly wasn't improving with the passage of time.

I bounced in and out of detox centers and hospitals for about the next year. I couldn't even begin to count the times my situation was considered hopeless by more people than just myself. I entered treatment again in the fall of 1987. I was having thoughts of suicide, and I was continually going on drinking binges. I knew I had to try to stop this madness or I was going to kill myself or go stark-raving mad. I was there about thirty days this time. Shortly after I got out, I got a job working with delinquent boys. It was something I considered an opportunity, considering my work history and my history of alcoholism.

I felt I had something to offer. I could give them lists of things not to do because my life had been one mistake after another.

I started drinking again within a week of getting the job. I never drank before work or at work, but I made up for lost time when I was done for the day. There were many days when it was very hard for me to get up and go to work, but my supply of alcohol depended on my paycheck. I couldn't contribute a great deal in my state of mind, but I managed to keep my job for about ten months.

I missed my son, and I planned a trip to Florida. I bought a motorcycle, and gave notice at work.

That was October 1988. I had been drunk and drugged every day except the time I spent in prison, jails, or treatment centers for twenty-four years.

I headed out on my motorcycle with everything I owned. I was going to Orlando, Florida, where my son was living at the time. When I arrived, all I got when I called his home was an answering machine. I had let Nancy know I was coming, so I assumed she had decided not to make it easy for me to see John. I tried to get through on the phone for several hours. I finally got mad and decided to head for Naples, Florida. I knew a place where I could stay for a while until I figured out what I was going to do. I knew a young couple who had lived in the town where I had operated my pre-school. We had gotten along real well before they had moved to Florida, so they were willing to put up with me long enough for me to find work.

I got a job as a chauffeur and cook for a wealthy couple in Naples. Cooking had been a hobby of mine throughout my life, so I was fairly skilled in that area. It was a good job with opportunity, but my ambition was non-existent. I lived on their boat that was docked nearby and spent every night after work getting drunk. I would drink on the job occasionally. Everyone else was always drinking something

> I was sitting there when my ego suggested that I was a rather remarkable person. Immediately a voice said, "The only thing remarkable about you is that you are not dead!"

alcoholic, so no one noticed the smell of alcohol on me. I was making $300 a week and living on their boat for free. It would have been a good opportunity to save some money and get my life together, but the pull of alcohol was too strong; work interfered with my drinking. I left without giving my employers notice. I was headed back to Orlando to see my son; I missed him.

When I got to Orlando, I called and Nancy answered the phone. She said I could see John if I decided to stay in the area. I did some temporary work until I finally got a job doing maintenance at an apartment complex. The job paid seven dollars an hour, just barely enough to just get by in Florida. The job was all right, but the woman who managed the apartment complex loved to gossip. She was always talking about someone in the complex, and she never had anything good to say about anyone. She made me sick with her gossip, as if life is not tough enough. I quit after a couple of months and headed back to Minnesota for the summer.

I had some visits with my son, so I felt as if I had at least established contact with him. I wanted him to know his father. And most important, I wanted him to know how much I loved him. He was at an age where he knew of my alcoholism: I'm sure it was hard on him, but we were still able to tell each other we loved one another.

I didn't have anything to go back to in St. Cloud, except a few family members; and with my addictions and attitude, it was hard for them to be enthusiastic in their greetings. They put up with me because I was part of their family, not for any other reason.

I had everything I owned with me on my motorcycle. My saddle bags and a duffel bag held the remainder of my worldly possessions. I only had about $150 to my name, nowhere to live, and no job. I didn't have much to show for 41 years of life.

I stayed around St. Cloud for a while, hanging out at the bars and drinking all my money away. After about two weeks, my money was gone, and I was staying wherever I could when I needed sleep. I borrowed a little money and got on my bike and headed north. I thought I would visit a couple of people I knew, maybe find some work, or figure out how to get some cash.

I stopped at a bar to have a few drinks and decided I might as well try a little gambling; I really didn't have much to lose. I won $400 in about fifteen minutes and had the sense not to continue gambling that day. I had a small nest egg now; I figured by living in my tent and taking it reasonably easy with my drinking, I could make that money last a few weeks. I never planned any further ahead than that.

These were some of the lowest times I can remember. I drank around the clock, slept when I had to, and got up and did it again. None of my past friends wanted anything to do with me. I was quite different than I had been when I owned and operated the pre-school. At least I had paid my own way. Now I was a bum, inside and out. My life was a vast emptiness; I sensed my loneliness very deeply.

I got a little too drunk one rainy night. I had been drinking at a bar since about ten in the morning that day. I left there about ten in the evening; I barely remember it now. It was dark and raining. A car was coming up behind me very fast, and I figured I would just move over to the right a little bit and let him pass. I moved my motorcycle toward the right and looked back over my left shoulder to see if the car had enough room to pass me. In the process, I hit the curb. I don't remember anything after that until I woke up in the hospital.

I came to in the emergency room briefly. Someone told me I had been in an accident, and the doctor asked me how much I had to drink. He said I was going to be there for a while and he wanted to know if I was going to go through withdrawal from alcohol. He knew who I was from the time I had been through treatment at their hospital a few years before. I told him I would be going through withdrawal. I knew I would get more drugs to help me "come down."

I came to again when I had been moved to a private room in the hospital. The doctor was there, and he told me I had broken most of the ribs on the right side of my chest, and one of the broken ribs had punctured my lung. He told me he had to insert a metal tube through my chest into my lung so my lung could be re-inflated. I was not given any pain killer for this process because they didn't know my blood alcohol level, and giving pain killers to someone who had a lot of alcohol in their system might kill him. So I had to bear the pain of having that metal tube pushed through my chest. The doctor told me I had some other injuries as well as the broken ribs, but they were not considered as serious.

I did not regain consciousness until some time later. When I did come to, apparently I had gotten out of bed and was wandering the halls of the hospital. I remember a nurse leading me back to my room. I did not know it was a hospital room; it seemed to me to be some kind of camper. I remember asking the nurse if it was her place, and she said it was. I told her it was really nice. She helped me into bed, and then a group of nurses strapped me down to the bed so I couldn't move.

I remember waiting until they had left the room, thinking I was securely tied down. I began to work the straps loose, and I was almost free when a nurse looked in the door of my room and saw what I was up to. Then all I remember is being surrounded by people holding me down and securing the straps more firmly around my body. I didn't know who they were. I was scared and confused. Then I felt at least two different needles in me and the lights went out.

I woke up sometime later and tried to get free. When I couldn't get the straps loose, I began yelling like a madman. They tried to calm me down by giving me something that knocked me out for about two days. When I came to, I had been in the hospital for about five days.

I had obviously had some bad reactions to the mixture of medicines they had given me. I had never had any similar experiences when I had gone through withdrawal from alcohol and drugs. I always had been aware of my surroundings.

I demanded they release me. My system was craving alcohol and nicotine. They tried to talk me out of going, and they told me I had pneumonia in my right lung and my ribs had not healed enough for me to be moving around. They were afraid of a lawsuit if they kept me, and a lawsuit if they released me. They finally had me sign a paper releasing them from all responsibility.

Someone brought me the clothes that had been cut off me when I was admitted. That was all I had to wear. So, I left the hospital at about nine o'clock at night dressed in cut-off jeans, a ripped shirt, socks, and tennis shoes. Both of my eyes were blackened and my face was covered with cuts and bruises. My whole body was covered with cuts and abrasions. I hadn't eaten because I had been unconscious and was fed intravenously for five days. I was quite a sight.

My plan was to get a pint of liquor, some cigarettes, and begin to hitchhike back to St. Cloud, about 60 miles away. If I couldn't find a ride, I would sleep in the ditch. It turned out I was just a few minutes late getting to the liquor store; it had just closed.

I went to a bar next door to get a drink and some cigarettes. Someone who knew me came up to me with an astonished look on her face and asked me what had happened. I explained briefly what had happened. She called someone she knew who used to be a friend of mine to see if she could find a place for me to stay until morning. I could tell from the lengthy conversation that she was having a tough time talking this fellow into letting me stay at his house. He didn't want anything to do with me. He had watched my decline over the last couple of years. I knew he didn't need someone like me asking him for help in the midst of my continuing crises.

She finally talked him into letting me stay with him that night, so she gave me a ride over there. I was still real drugged up from the hospital, and I had been drinking to get rid of my craving for alcohol. I talked to my friend when I got over to his house, but I'm sure I didn't make much sense. He just humored me until I fell asleep from the effects of the drugs and alcohol. In the morning, he gave me a ride back to my mother's house in St. Cloud, more to get rid of me than for any other reason. I couldn't blame him a bit. I made myself sick. Why should my affect on others be any different?

I arrived at my mother's house, and she took one look at

me and asked me why I hadn't stayed at the hospital. I told her they were like a bunch of mad scientists who had bought a building and opened it under the pretext of it being a hospital. She didn't buy it.

She felt sorry for me and allowed me to stay there for a few days. But I was continually borrowing money from her for cigarettes and booze. She had enough trouble just taking care of herself on her fixed income. She didn't need me draining her meager savings.

My situation had never been worse. I had no money, no clothing (my saddle bags had been stolen from my motorcycle after the accident but before the police arrived) and no job. Even if I could have worked, I had nowhere I could call home, and no friends, no vehicle, and no driver's license, and several hundred dollars in fines for DUI, and my motorcycle was destroyed. To say my situation was bleak would be a definite understatement.

One of my brothers knew how hard it was on my mother having me stay with her and told me I could stay with him if I quit drinking. I agreed; I needed a place to stay, but I had no intention of quitting drinking. I would just do my drinking elsewhere; all I needed was a place to sleep. This routine went on for about a month.

14 The doorway to hell is always open.

ANGING OUT AT A COUPLE OF THE rougher bars in St. Cloud, I met a lot of people who were in a similar situation as mine. I ran into some people I had known years before; now they were full-blown alcoholics. Everybody was hustling everybody else for drugs, a drink, or a place to stay. Even though most of these people were alcoholics, they would help each other out when they could. I saw more sharing and unselfish giving among these "drunks" than I had anywhere else in my travels. They helped me feel as though I was around friends when I was down at the bars drinking with them. The bar, in effect, became my home. I got there when it opened, and I was there when it closed. And I would make sure ahead of time that I would have some liquor stashed away for the time in between. I could usually find a place to sleep when the bar closed. It was kind of a strange sight. There was always a group of people looking for a place to stay as closing time approached; about a third of us usually had nowhere to go.

I got to know the owner of one of the bars pretty well; after all, I had become a fixture of sorts in there. She offered me a job as a bartender. I snatched it up. I would open the bar in the morning and work until about six in the evening. It gave me plenty of time to drink anything I wanted while I was at work, and as a result of working there, I had a tab. There were nights when I would sleep on the pool table because I didn't have anywhere else to stay. I met a lot of people through bartending, some good, some bad. But I had at least developed some superficial friendships which helped me feel less alone. I could walk in anytime and find someone I knew to sit and drink with.

Then people started dying. First, it was a fellow I had known pretty well who had been a regular at the bar. He was killed in a car accident. Next a couple of the older regular customers died. A friend of mine died from combining alcohol and barbiturates. Someone else got stabbed. Another fellow I knew pretty well just got a little bit too discouraged and killed himself with a shotgun blast to his head. A friend's sister who I had grown up with died as the result of liver damage from excessive alcohol use. It seemed there was a funeral every six or eight weeks. Death was the consequence of living the way we were; we all knew we could be next. We lived for the moment. We didn't feel there was any other reason to live.

Eventually, the bar closed down and we all moved to another one a few doors down. This was another rough place, with the same type of clientele as our previous "home away from home." We alcoholics would hit the bar stools at 8 o'clock in the morning, shaking until we got those first two or three drinks in us. Then we would just sit and talk or watch the television. There wasn't much conversation the first couple of hours until people started feeling better. By mid-afternoon, the place was usually full. This bar came as a shock to some of the unsuspecting college students who happened to find it. They were used to well-dressed, fairly polite people who just went out to have a good time. They were not ready for the down and dirty crowd of rowdies that for the most part lived at this particular bar. If you were not known in this place, you didn't feel very welcome. There were many people who walked in the front door and just continued walking right out the back door, thanking God they made it through the maze of drunks without incident.

Usually someone would have a joint of marijuana, and we would just go in the bathroom to smoke it. Everyone was used to the smell of pot filtering through the place. The bartenders were supposed to make sure no one used drugs in the bar, but for the most part, they just joined in. If they didn't, there wasn't a thing they could do about it. No one was willing to risk his life by calling the police. Fights were fairly common; alcohol tends to make a person feel braver than he really is, or just plain stupid.

The police would generally walk through the place a couple of times a day. They didn't do that at any of the other bars in town, but they knew the class of people who hung out at this place. It was a constant headache for them. It was also a place where they were likely to find people wanted by the law. Every once in awhile someone would be assisted off his stool, handcuffed, and taken away.

During this time, I put myself in detox several times to come down from binge drinking. I also put myself in St. Cloud Hospital for treatment on several occasions. Most of the time I would just walk out after I had gone through the most serious effects of withdrawal. But I did try the program for treatment again, with no success. I had come to believe I was destined to be a drunk the rest of my life. I had no hope; why should anything change? Treatment for alcoholism didn't help, praying for this affliction to go away didn't help, relocating and starting over didn't help. I hated everything about life and what I had become. I was just hoping to die quietly and be put out of this constant misery I was caught up in. I considered those who had died as the fortunate ones; their hell had been terminated.

The new year of 1990 came and went. I continued to abuse drugs and alcohol. There was no reason for me to celebrate the new year; there was more cause for sadness than celebration. Several times during this year I attempted to stop drinking, but to no avail. I was in and out of several unhealthy relationships, which did nothing to make things easier. Loneliness would send me right back into the bottle; it was my biggest enemy. Trying to meet my very real needs with emotionally handicapped people like myself was like pouring gasoline on a blazing fire.

Suicide became a daily thought running through my mind. I actually found solace in that thought. I felt like my life had been a series of continuous falls, and, with each additional fall, I was becoming more and more damaged and hurt. I was running out of the strength it took to get up; it seemed pointless. I was tired of the fight. I just wanted to rest, but I could find no rest.

It was about this time that I met a woman who seemed relatively stable compared to the rest of the crowd. We talked and found we liked things about each other. She was quite a bit younger than I was, but it didn't seem to make any difference to either one of us. We spent quite a bit of time together. She was aware of the problems I had with alcohol, and even though she seldom drank, she seemed to know about the hopelessness I was fighting. She lifted me emotionally and gave me hope for the first time in years.

We talked about getting an apartment together and settling down. I started looking for a job so I could get a place to live. I was staying with a woman, but things were real rough in that relationship, and I wanted out. It was just a place to stay. I cared for the person I was staying with, but I didn't love her nor did I think we were good for each other. We had slowly destroyed any trust that had been present when we first met. I kept looking for work, but with my work history, or the lack of it, I was unable to find a job right away.

I continued seeing the woman I had just met. We used to sit on the banks of the river and plan our future. She was an extremely sensitive woman, and she seemed much more mature in her thinking than most people her age. She was quiet and kept to herself quite a bit. She was always doing things to help other people out. She gave them rides or helped them move, or just listened to their troubles. She seemed almost out of place here, like an angel from somewhere far away.

In October, 1990, she was killed when a train struck the car she was riding in. The driver was drunk and survived the accident. He was later charged and is now in prison.

My world collapsed a little more inside me. No one had known of our relationship, or at least the intensity of it, so I couldn't share my sorrow with anyone. What would they care anyway? My despair, my anger, my resentment, and my pain grew.

I walked around drunk and in a daze for a few weeks.

Then I saw an ad in the paper for a job that I thought I might be able to get. It was hard, dirty work, the kind of job no one else wants. The choices I had at that time were very simple: I either killed myself or made another attempt at survival. I applied for the job. I was hired and went to work the following week. It would at least give me money to support my drinking habit.

The job I got was tearing out and removing old machinery. There were two of us hired to do this work. The other fellow had experienced drinking problems in his life, but he seemed to have things under control. It was nice to be able to work so closely with someone that had experienced many of the same things that I was dealing with. He gave me support when I needed it. Now I began really struggling to stop drinking. I had several weeks of sobriety and then I got angry about something and began drinking again. I seemed to be drawn into drinking when I felt lonely, or angry, or just discouraged about my situation. But it was a struggle for me, and my continuing failures only reinforced my belief that I was destined to be a drunk all my life.

I got involved in a relationship, but it suffered a great deal because of the problems we both had. There were several times I started drinking in response to a conflict in the relationship. There were many conflicts. I had become so needy that I was totally miserable when I did not have that other person I thought I needed to make me complete. I knew that if I had any hope at all for my life to change, it would take a miracle, and I didn't expect one of those.

After I had been on the job for a few months, I injured my back and also discovered I had a hernia. Through examination, I found out I had a bulging disc in my back. The doctor also recommended surgery for my hernia. So I was out of commission for a while. Too much free time for me was not what I needed in my life. It became very tempting to drink because of all the time on my hands.

After I had been drinking heavily for a week or ten days, without eating anything, I would be in rough shape. I signed myself into detox on several occasions. When a person goes into detox, the staff requires that they change into pajamas to prevent them from leaving the detox center. I left detox dressed only in pajamas on three different occasions. It was at night, so I didn't have to embarrass myself completely by walking three miles home in pajamas.

I had problems when I started coming down off alcohol. I would be filled with fear and terror. If I was not given some medication to help me relax, I had a great deal of difficulty going through withdrawal from the alcohol. People who have not experienced this terror cannot even imagine what it can be like. Unfortunately, there are still some people involved in the rehabilitation efforts that feel people who put themselves in the position of being alcoholic should suffer through the effects of withdrawal. They think it might teach the alcoholic a lesson. These are people who do not understand and do not know about the word "compassion." They should be in another line of work.

Throughout the spring and summer, I kept trying to take control of my life, but I continued experiencing failure. I would end up binge-drinking constantly. I just didn't care anymore. I was in and out of the detox center and St. Cloud Hospital on many occasions to try and get some help, but I could not find what it was that was causing this crumbling of my life. I could not control my drinking. I might stay sober for a few weeks, but then I would get upset about something or become discouraged and then I'd end up back down at the bar trying to get rid of the loneliness and despair I was feeling. It seemed to be an endless cycle of hell.

In the early fall of 1991, I committed myself to a state hospital hoping I could come down from the alcohol without having to go through the madness I had to pass through to get back to reality.

They did not have a detox center at this hospital; but after I told the sheriff's deputy that had driven me there that I was considering suicide, they admitted me. They had to put me in a locked ward which was home to many very disturbed people. This place was where the seriously mentally ill people were housed for the safety of the community. It was an experience I will never forget. There were people in straight jackets, people who would suddenly lose control of their minds. In its own way, it was enlightening for me, but it was difficult to think of the enlightenment when I saw what had caused it. These people did not have any choice about their situation. They were locked up because they could not fit into society. They did not choose to live like that. I felt somewhat ashamed that I, someone who *did* have a choice, was there taking the staff's time away from those who really needed it. It was an unsettling place to be. If a patient "flipped out," someone sounded an alarm and staff members from all parts of the building would rush to help with an out-of-control situation. Ten or twelve people would arrive in a matter of seconds. Their security was efficient, I imagine, out of necessity.

I was in the hospital for several days until they thought I had gone through the worst effects of withdrawal. I thought the staff was extremely compassionate, considering their responsibilities. They were truly dealing with lost souls.

I went back home very grateful for the help I had received at the hospital. It was November and the holidays were fast approaching. I had come to dread the holidays because it seemed they were a time for family, fun, and friends. My life consisted of loneliness, isolation, and despair. It was hard to feel any happiness around others when my life was filled with so much dread.

Through the efforts of my ex-wife Nancy, my son, John, who was 12 years old at that time, came for a visit over the Thanksgiving holiday. He had been living in Florida with his mother all this time. It was really good to see him. I didn't drink at all while he was visiting me; I didn't want to spoil his happiness while he was here. But when he left, I made up for lost time and got stinking drunk for about a week before I decided to put myself into the detox center.

I went in to detox on Friday and left Sunday afternoon feeling somewhat better than I had when I had gone in.

I went home to my small, one-room apartment. I sat there that Sunday evening, and I just could not go on like this anymore, but I knew I could not change things. I had tried and tried. I got down on my knees, and with sincerity, I asked God to come into

my life and help me because I couldn't take any more of this punishment. I had done it my way all my life and I was the worst person I knew. I was totally out of resources and drained of life. I
could see where, with every move, I had destroyed my life piece by
piece. I didn't know if God was real, but I knew that I was done
doing it my way.

My life changed overnight; it was December 1, 1991.

Part 2

We are being drawn
from the darkness
by angels of God.

15 The fact that something is difficult to believe does not make it any less true.

HAT YOU ARE ABOUT TO READ ON the following pages is true. I have not embellished any of the experiences I am about to relate to the reader in order to make them more spectacular than they were. These experiences are difficult to believe because they are not common ones; rather, they are supernatural experiences which completely changed my life and altered forever, in a very dramatic way, the path I was on. There are some readers who, unfortunately, will not be able to accept these occurrences as real. And there are those who will believe them without question. I can only tell you what happened. I cannot make you believe. I assure you, I would not presume to add pages to a book the Lord gave me. I would be content in His word and would not attempt to improve upon His word, thinking that I might gloss over the truth to improve upon what I received.

My experiences began with a surrender, then came joy, inner-peace, and love. Then I experienced God's supernatural power, and I realized things were not as they appeared to be. I received knowledge I had not had access to before. I was continually drawn deeper and deeper into this process until it had impressed me with such intensity that it became, in effect, my whole life.

I began to experience what seemed like revelations of particular pieces of knowledge, moments when my intellect received information as a complete thought or explanation. It was not something I heard. It was something I knew, something intuitive, like a light going on inside of me. It was as if someone gave me a beautiful plant; and at the moment I received that plant, I not only saw its beauty, but I understood its origin, its function, and its purpose. I received internal visions of beauty which continue to this day when I am in prayer, usually in the recitation of the Holy Rosary.

When I say "internal vision," it is something I see internally when my eyes are closed in prayer. These visions are very clear and well defined, and I have never experienced anything like them before in my life. They are not part of my imagination, but part of God's creativity working in my life. The beauty I have seen is truly indescribable: I have seen nothing on earth to which I can compare the beauty of these visions.

My entire perception began to change as doors and windows of existence were flung open to reveal a world I had never imagined. It is interesting to note that all of the same inconsistencies that were present in my youth which caused me to react so negatively to this world were still present. It is only my perception and understanding which had changed. The errors I had made in my life became obvious; obvious, too, were the answers to correct my errors. I now understood how important faith, trust, and perseverance were in replacing my ignorance. My new insights helped on a daily basis with all obstacles in my path. I learned lessons intuitively without having to suffer the consequences of trial and error. God was extremely merciful in my stumbling attempts to change engrained behavior. The lonely void, which had been my constant companion throughout my entire life, was filled to overflowing with the love of God.

My most precious moments were those shared only with God in contemplative prayer. The experience was like being drawn into a huge funnel of love; as this funnel narrowed, as I was drawn further into it, I found it necessary to undergo spiritual change to continue through this process of discovering love and truth. God's love has the effect of removing debris like a strainer. As we are poured through the strainer, the goodness goes through, but the impurities and imperfections stay inside the basket. In the refining process, I had to surrender my pre-conceived ideas about everything. It was then that I saw the truth.

When I say I "saw" these things, I mean it literally. When a concept was presented to me, I understood it immediately. With each new lesson I took time to experience, digest, and utilize what I had learned. This period of time generally lasted about fourteen days.

These things came to me through the grace of God that I might begin to understand why I was here. I consider what has happened to me as a blessing. It is not something I deserved and I do not consider myself special in any way. I believe that I was made anew that the Lord might be glorified in my healing. I never in my life considered that I  might someday be writing this book. I never in my wildest dreams thought I would come to experience such dramatic and consistent events which would draw me down the path to God. I have always been the skeptic, the one who needed proof, the "doubting Thomas" in the Bible. I had to put my fingers into the wounds of Christ to believe. The power of Christ's blood moved through me, covered me, and cleansed me and began to make me a new person.

During this process, I did not spend a great deal of time reading and studying the Bible. I spent time with it, but the truths I experienced came through the Spirit of God. The only things required of me were faith, trust, and a sincerity of purpose. God continually answered my prayers, often going far beyond what I would have been happy with. I experienced joy, a new feeling for me—a feeling of such intense love that I would rather die than give it up.

I did not achieve wholeness; it is a continuing process. But it is a process I anticipate each and every day. God's love caused me to love Him so strongly in return that I welcomed the opportunities for growth that He gave me. I continue to face difficulties in my life just like everyone else, but it seems I am receiving an abundance of God's help and guidance. And those difficulties appear to be very dramatically overcome through the use of *prayer*. That appears to be the starting point: to approach God humbly and with *sincerity* in our heart, for that is where He dwells, once we have asked Him to *take control* of our lives.

I do not look at this as my opportunity alone. It is an opportunity for all of us who value goodness and love. God hears all prayers, and returns the sincere love given Him in prayers. Praying is not something we try for a week or two; it is something we do. Our faith and involvement in becoming what God wants us to become is what makes prayer work. We must allow the changes that occur in us, which God's love brings us, to develop and flourish. For it is through these changes that we are allowed to see and experience the truth about our purpose here.

I would never misrepresent what I have experienced; it would make those things valueless. It would destroy and distort the message. I do not have that right. I believe if God felt I would ever take my hand from His, He wouldn't have taken my hand to begin with. The presence of God in any relationship always promotes mutual trust, because of His nature. God shares his love and it is reciprocal because of its overwhelming, unmistakable power.

God will allow us to win, to understand. He will not, however, prevent us from losing. The choice is ours.

16 I was brought from emptiness into the midst of heaven with a single prayer; in a quiet hour, on a silent night, I was enveloped by the love of God.

 HEN I AWOKE THE NEXT MORN-ing, December 2, 1991, I felt something very powerful and evil had been drawn from my being. My attitude began to change as things appeared different to me. This recognition was a gradual process. I found myself drawn to prayer. I felt a long-ing I could not fill any other way. I felt assured that everything was going to be all right. There was no need to worry about things; they seemed to be taking care of themselves. This newfound confidence was hard to accept since I was very used to doing things my way, constantly planning, worry-ing, and attempting to anticipate my disasters before I came upon them. I was learning that if I left things alone and simply prayed, I need not worry. From that day until this day, I still stumble and have occasional doubts about the reality of my experiences; but I realize this is the "human" part of me. God has *never* let me down and I rely on faith to propel me forward.

Some of my immediate problems began to disappear. For one, my financial situation was extremely poor, but money began to come to me from various people, places, or situations which I had not anticipated. It was not a lot of money, but it helped to meet my current needs.

I felt drawn to church. It was as though I had tasted some-thing very sweet and wonderful, and I found myself drawn back to it for more—very much like my old addictions, only this one did not require drugs, and what I was feeling was very real.

I always went to church when there would be the fewest

people around because I felt uncomfortable in crowds. I was battling with the concept of the reality of God. Something had changed inside me, and it was beginning to change me on the outside. It was so hard to believe that God was there. Even though I could not see Him, I felt He was there in Spirit with me. In the beginning, I chalked a lot of things off to coincidence, but the coincidences didn't seem to let up.

My relationships with my family, friends, and even strangers began to improve. I saw things I never saw in people before. I had always considered myself very able to "read" people. I had developed this technique from my way of living; I was a confidence man. I had to be able to anticipate people's behavior living the kind of life I had lived. But…I began to realize there was much more to life now than before. When I looked into the faces of friends, family, and strangers, I saw the fear, the anger, the loneliness, the despair, and the hatred; but I also saw the goodness, the kindness, the hope, the love, and the desire for God.

All of my insight was very gradual because of the interior battles I had to fight. The "old Tom" wanted to continue to be in control.

Throughout December, I continued to pray very often. After I prayed, I felt at peace—a feeling I came to know as God's love for me. In the third week of December on a Sunday evening, I turned out the lights and lit a candle on a small altar I had been using to pray in front of before I went to bed. I began to feel the presence of someone with me. I immediately felt enveloped in a warm, safe, and extremely loving feeling. Although I felt warm, I was covered with goose bumps; it was as though a cloud filled with God's love descended from above. I was filled with absolute joy, peace, and love. It was something I had never experienced before. I was in complete awe of what was happening to me.

About a week before Christmas, I had finished my prayers and gotten into bed and suddenly, but very gently, I felt an arm go around me as if to comfort me. I lay there, and I was immediately filled with a sense of complete trust and peace. I did not merely *imagine* someone's arm going around me. I had just climbed into bed, so it was not a dream. The feeling did not frighten me; I remember only that feeling of peace, security and love, and I fell instantly asleep. I knew it was a sign to assure me that what I had been experiencing was real, that there was no need to worry about anything. Although it would be some time before I would discover how thorough God's love and promises really were, I was "hooked." I had to believe and accept my experiences, or I was becoming psychotic. Those were my choices.

> Our movement forward is hindered only by our choices. We should look back only to recall a lesson well learned, and move forward with that thought as the correct motivation for our next decision.

I lived in a small efficiency apartment on the fourth floor of a large, old remodeled building. It was as though a supernatural presence had moved in with me. I began to feel warm breezes moving around me as I moved about my apartment. I was also filled with a sense of not being alone. I really got the sense that there were wings of angels around me. At times when I did not have my TV or stereo on, I heard angelic choirs singing very softly as though coming to me from a great distance. My apartment was filled with plants and warm colors, and at night I light candles and pray, but now there was a presence that had not been there before. It was not a presence that made me uneasy, it was a very comforting, loving feeling. That feeling was very intense; there was nothing subtle about it. I am very aware of it when it comes over me; it is so wonderful—it takes all thoughts to another place, except those of God.

A few days before Christmas, I lit a candle and knelt to pray. As soon as I began to pray, I had a beautiful vision of a choir of angels who were singing and praising God; and I understood the choir was singing because I had come to God in prayer. They were celebrating my surrender to God. The vision lasted only a few moments, but I will never forget how beautiful it was and how real it seemed. Christmas had formerly been very lonely and empty for me for many years. But this Christmas was different; I knew the joy of Christmas for the first time in my life. I was filled with a sense of assurance, with peace, with feelings there are not words for.

> I had become a leaf in the winds of God, gently moved from place to place by whispers of the spirit.

On Christmas Eve our family gathered at my brother's apartment for a dinner and to sit around the Christmas tree and talk. I couldn't share my experiences because no one would believe me. Nothing had changed much on the outside of myself, but inside, everything was in turmoil. They all thought I was just in a good mood for a change. I remember sitting there looking at these people for what seemed the first time. I saw the depth of their individual personalities. I was amazed at my sudden awareness of their complexities. I began to realize how little I really knew, although I had thought I was the man with all the answers.

I told my family I was going to midnight Mass, which surprised them. I left quickly, not wanting to give them an explanation for my sudden change of behavior. I think I was afraid to say anything for fear my joyful feelings were temporary and my life would soon revert to its formal bleak routine. I used my mother's car to drive to church because I didn't have one (I had lost everything I owned except for some clothing and the few things I had in my small apartment). I had to cross over the Mississippi River bridge to get to church; and as I did, it was as though I had entered a different place. The skies were layered with clouds that stretched from the rooftops into the sky. It actually looked like a stairway to heaven. There were no people, no cars, just peace and quiet. The church was only a few blocks away after I crossed the river and there was not a soul to be seen anywhere. I got to the church only to find there was no midnight Mass service. The church was locked, and the parking lot was empty. I looked up at the sky; and it was, without question, the most beautiful sight I had ever seen in the skies. The clouds stretched from the rooftops to the skies; it appeared I could have walked up this stairway if I had wanted to. I drove slowly back to our family gathering wondering what was going on in my life.

When I arrived back at my brother's apartment, I tried to tell my mother and brothers and sisters about the sky, but no one would listen. They were joking and talking among themselves, celebrating Christmas with a few traditional drinks. No one paid any attention to what I was saying. After I had become more persistent, they started joking about it saying things like, "Sure, Tom, there's a stairway out there." They were used to my usual drugged and drunken state of mind. No one took me seriously. I was sure there would be something on the radio about the sky the next morning. I told them they would be sorry if they didn't go out to see this phenomenon. But there wasn't anything on the radio the next day, and no one I talked to had seen what I saw. It was as though I had been given that gift of beauty for my act of faith of going out on that cold wintry night to celebrate the birth of Jesus.

I felt like there were angels living with me during the last days of December. I felt a constant presence; and when I knelt down to pray, I was enveloped by a cloud of love. I was drawn into prayer more and more often during the day. I would examine my experiences for flaws or inconsistencies. It had been just too difficult for me to imagine that God was real, that something far better existed beyond this place. I always had hope; but to accept it as being real was very difficult when I couldn't see or hear anything that would give me proof. I had always been a skeptic, but this time I could not find inconsistencies.

> It is not our job to *understand,* but simply to be in *unity* with Christ.

On Sunday, January 5, 1992, at about seven in the evening, I knelt down in prayer. I was holding a "Pardon Crucifix," which I had bought the day before at a Christian bookstore, the first religious item I had ever owned. As I began my prayers, I sensed the same intense presence I had felt when I knelt in prayer before. Again I was covered with goose bumps but, at the same time, filled with the warmth and security I felt when I was reaching out to God. When I got to the end of the Lord's Prayer, I began hearing a crackling sound, like static electricity—similar to the sound you hear when you take a sweater out of the drier. It started slowly but then built up to a crescendo of energy rushing into the crucifix. I pulled my hands to my chest holding the crucifix and said, "My God." I was filled with heat, and the crucifix was almost too hot to hold. I was filled with fear and awe at the power of this occurrence.

I sat in that spot for two hours, not moving, evaluating my entire life. I was at the same time filled with the knowledge of God. I prayed and thanked Him for how He was changing my life.

I found out later that this particular Sunday was celebrated as the Feast Day of the Epiphany, the day Christ revealed Himself to the world. It is an interesting coincidence that on such a special day God reached out and touched this drunkard, this emotional cripple, changing my life forever.

I began to see a therapist I had known through the years. He had overcome great hardships in his own life; and, as a result, he had become a very spiritual person. I felt that I needed some guidance in light of my experiences. I needed to talk to someone who could help me understand them. I consider it *no accident* that I sought out Ed for help. He was exactly the kind of man I needed for this journey I had just begun. I spent quite a bit of time with him, seeing him at least once a week and sometimes more often. He never charged me for his time; it was almost as if we had a job to do together. I had some questions; he had some answers. No one could have answered my questions more thoroughly. He was very aware of my past, since we had known each other for thirty years.

The Longing

I have been alone
among the jagged rock
humanity calls home,
and seen, and felt,
its emptiness and loneliness;
and then I was held
in the arms of God,
and I understood the word love
and all that it contains;
and I understood this is not my home,
and with each beat of my heart
my longing grows
to be held again,
but this time...
forever.

Written April, 1994.

In the evening, I spent much of my time thinking about my experiences and praying for guidance. The atmosphere of my apartment had begun to change as well. I acquired a variety of books dealing with God and religion. My altar began to grow crowded with different religious statues, medals, and symbols. I began reading the Bible and other books dealing with the saints, the apparitions of Mary, and books about other people whose lives had been changed by their own encounters with God. I felt absolutely drawn to spiritual enlightenment: I had a great hunger for more of it. I was 43 years old, and I thought I had experienced everything significant in life. But now, everything was changing—*everything!*

I began to do helpful things for others, to be more loving and giving, to be more polite, considerate and patient. I found out how difficult it was doing nice things for others and not telling anyone about it (before, I had always sought praise from others because I needed it so badly). I was so used to doing things my way, and now I had to release that selfishness and accept significant changes in my life. It sounded easy enough, but engrained behavior has all the rigidity that its name implies. I was extremely set in my ways, so it was a battle all the way, but I found I had someone mighty powerful helping me. On my own, I did not have the strength to make the changes to improve my life, I was too far gone. I decided to count on God. In one of my discussions with Ed, he pointed out that I had taken the first three steps that AA believes are necessary for a person with an addiction problem to begin the recovery process.

> ### A A Steps 1, 2 & 3
> We admitted we were powerless over alcohol—that our lives had become unmanageable.
> We came to believe that a power greater than ourselves could restore us to sanity.
> We made a decision to turn our will and our lives over to the care of God as we understood Him.

I simply cannot say enough about the dramatic effects of this decision on my life. I was a changed person. It was going to be a continuing journey through all twelve steps of AA for the next three years.

As little as I liked the sound of the old cliché "born again," I had to admit that it was the best way to describe what had happened to me. When my son was about 2-years-old, I would sometimes call him "Kleinschmidt" just for fun. He would respond by laughing and saying, "I'm not that guy." Well, I wasn't that guy that used to live in this body. That guy, Tom, who used to be such a jerk—I'm not him any more. And it was the despair that was turned to hope, the sadness that had changed to joy, and my path that had turned toward God that had allowed my life to be touched so thoroughly by Him. It had been my surrender. And I do not believe it could have been done any other way. I do not believe those three steps are a separate process; they require one another to be effective. The third step was always the most difficult for me, because of my pride.

The contrast of what my life had been and what it was becoming was striking.

The more difficult our journey,
the more blessed we become
for our efforts.

17 God does interior design.

N JANUARY 19, 1992, I WAS IN PRAYER with my arms stretched out above me. I had prayed for a particular thing to happen in my life and was in the process of completing the prayer when I heard what sounded like a ball of fire come down from above me, and I felt it enter my chest filling me with heat. The sound was exactly like the sound you would hear if you took a burning torch and swung it through the air quickly, or the sound of a flaming arrow shot through the air.

I was again struck with the power and the magnificence of God. These things just didn't happen to people! I was stunned. I could not understand why my life was being affected so dramatically. I had spent some time with Ed discussing my experiences. He suggested I talk to a priest whom we both knew. I did as he suggested and became more comfortable within myself. Both men had told me that I should not place my exterior experiences above the interior work being done in me by the Lord. God wanted my attention, and He got it.

> AA STEP 4
> We make a searching and fearless moral inventory of ourselves.

I found myself beginning to develop a new personality. At the age of 43, I had never developed solid values. I was not a "mature adult" by any stretch of the imagination. My attitude had

---

been that of a selfish child. This newfound realization continued to shock me the more I became aware of it. I had been the man with all the answers! Now I realized that I had none. It was a humbling experience. I had tried to be my own god, and had ultimately discovered the depth of my ignorance. God had let me live in my delusion until I became profoundly dissatisfied with it; only then, through much stumbling and falling down, would I be able to change course and be able to learn and grow.

I began listening to Christian radio stations. The music seemed to fill a need in me. I found the music beautiful and inspiring. During the previous three or four years of my life, I had stopped listening to music because it would fill me with a sadness and emptiness. Music touched my soul, and my soul hurt very badly before I experienced God's love. I had actually detached myself from music. It was as though the music touched raw nerves that had become exposed. I had become an emotional basket case by the time I turned to God.

February came, and I began looking forward to spring. For the first time in my life I felt as though there really was hope. I felt like a child. Every experience with people became a learning experience. Every day was filled with small revelations about how completely wrong I had been in my first judgment about a person or a situation. I was starting at square one with another chance at life. I felt like I had been truly blind, and now I was beginning to see the light.

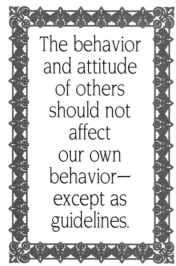

The behavior and attitude of others should not affect our own behavior—except as guidelines.

My craving for alcohol left me completely. At difficult times, although the thought of drinking entered my head, it seemed only to stir up those old feelings of fear and dread. I had no memories of fun or pleasure from drinking. The very thought of it made me feel sick, both physically and emotionally. I was very thankful for the bad images because I was afraid that I would need a great deal of self-discipline to quit drinking, and I had very little of that. I was on furlough from hell; I didn't want to go back.

On February 14, 1992, I was in prayer when I experienced the same sound and heat in the crucifix as on January 5. Once again, I was filled with fear and awe. It seemed as though I was being drawn closer to the Lord. I believe it happened to increase my faith and my trust. I was paying close attention to detail in my life now; things seemed to be happening for a reason. "Meaningful" coincidence began to be an everyday event. Ed reminded me often that I was only in the infant stage of growth, that I should not assume anything. I watched for the consistency in all things, and found it was there. In spite of my own weakness of faith, I found I could count on God, and that "all things [do] work together for good to them that love God, to them who are the called according to His purpose." Although at times it was hard to see what good could come from a particular situation, it always became clear to me at a later date.

> Often the answers I am given to my questions take several days, weeks, months, and even tears.

In March of 1992, I got a job driving nights for a delivery service. This job took me out of town each night, and I would generally be on the road for about six to eight hours a night. There was little contact with people and long hours on the road for prayer and meditation on God. It was a perfect opportunity for change and growth, and I made the best of it. I spent my days sleeping, so my contact with people was very limited; this solitude let me concentrate on what was happening inside me.

Not a day went by that I did not experience joy—not just happiness, but an all encompassing joy, a sense of peace and love beyond description. I did not even know a feeling like this existed. I had heard the word "joy," but I never knew what it was. Now I wondered how anyone who had this precious feeling could ever let it go.

I could not take my mind off God. I was drawn like a moth to a flame. If I wasn't in prayer, I was thinking about how wonderful everything was.

I couldn't share this intensity with many people; they didn't want to hear about it. Fortunately, I had Ed to talk to. He was interested and, I believe at times inspired by the changes he saw in me.

He would use the words "if this is real." I understood why he wondered. If I wasn't psychotic, if this revelation was real, it was extremely powerful and proved that there was something which we could not see but that really existed. And it was filled with goodness.

I remember early on when I was asking Ed why these things were happening to me. What was so special about me that I, of all people, would experience the love of God to this extent? He told me not to think too highly of myself. It may just be that I was so ignorant that God had to use a more intense means to reach me. Ed's observation helped to put things back into perspective for me.

In April of 1992, I turned 44. I could not help but feel I had spent my forty years in the wilderness. It was the first birthday that I felt there was any hope in my life. I had an honest job I liked. I was slowly growing up, and I was aware of the independence that I seemed to be gaining psychologically. I had always been very needy. I was plagued by loneliness, even when I was with people. But I lost this need for another person in my life as I began to become one with God through prayer. I learned that I need not depend on others for my happiness. All I really needed to make me complete was God. That dependence on others for happiness or fulfillment had been such a burden to me all my life. I did drugs and drank and did crazy things because I was lonely. I now began a process of healing, at the hands of the Holy Spirit; nothing else could have touched me like that and changed my life from despair and a total feeling of failure to the joy I was now filled with.

The months of May and June were months of continuing spiritual growth. I changed my priorities. I had been in a relationship with a woman off and on for a couple of years. It was strained and I felt it was best to bring the situation to an end. It was difficult to make that break with confidence, but I felt I must trust in God. So I ended the relationship.

I needed to concentrate on God, with no distractions. I welcomed the peace I felt with that decision. I had made a commitment to God, and trusted God to provide me with everything I needed.

Do not get the impression that I did not struggle with my faith from time to time; I am only human! But I saw such evidence in my day-to-day life, it would have been impossible for me to ignore the reality of God. As I had needs, He saw to them. When I felt lonely, He filled me with comfort and security. When I had a problem, I turned it over to God and I went on with what God wanted me to do. The problems virtually took care of themselves. God responded to my prayers every single time; although much of the time it was in ways I never expected.

> There is no bottom to hell, it goes on and on. We cannot expect the depth at which we suffer to end without acknowledging God and surrendering our will to Him.

During the first several months of these experiences, very often when I was in prayer, I would be deluged with curse words and evil thoughts. It was as though the evil left in me didn't want me to pray. It would sometimes confuse me with its overwhelming presence. I talked to Ed about this evil I sensed, and he told me it was something which I could expect. I should simply ignore the voices and steadfastly pray. I did as he told me. I gave the voices the importance they deserved—none. I don't recall when the "interference" stopped; it decreased gradually over a few months' time. It was not present at all after about seven or eight months.

That first year was primarily dedicated to spiritual growth and emotional maturity. As the summer passed into fall, I recognized the growth; but I was also impatient. In the beginning I thought this process of change would be easy: I'd just be a nice guy. But it was not as simple as that. I was struggling to change my responses to particular situations. Although the intent to change was there, so was the "old" behavior, the old responses. I realized eventually all I could do was my best, and then try to do better the next time. Although I saw progress, it seemed unbelievably slow. But I knew what I had been. You cannot take a piece of coal and expect it to change into a diamond overnight. Every struggle provided the opportunity for growth. It was my decision whether or not to accept and adapt to that growth. I began to understand the concept of free choice.

18

The true magnetic north of the human spirit is God.

INTER CAME AND EVEN THOUGH I had been alone for several months, I did not feel alone. My small apartment still seemed to hold a feeling of the presence of the Spirit of God. I always had the sense of the presence of angels when I was in prayer. It was just as though God gave me a heaven on earth. I was still very much aware of the evil in this world, much more than I had ever been; but my home felt safe and loving, and in some way was sheltering me from all of the terrible things in the world so that my growth could continue without interference. My priorities were internal now, not external. The world seemed incidental compared to what was going on inside of me.

My employer offered to sell me a company vehicle. Up until this time, I had been borrowing my mother's car to get to work. I felt very bad having to ask my mother for help. I was an adult. I told my employer I appreciated the offer, but there was no way I could afford to make the necessary payments. He offered to make the payments affordable, so I ended up with a fairly new vehicle with no down payment and very reasonable payments. It gave me more independence in my life and gave me a sense of security within myself. I was tired of only taking, never giving.

I was starting to develop a sense of pride in myself. It had been a long time since I had felt that way about anything I did. I wanted to change the image I projected toward others, but that change would prove to be much more difficult than I realized in the beginning. Just as my behavior had become engrained, so too had my reputation. It would take more than mere talk to convince others of any changes in my life. Ed gave me a line to think about: "You will know them by the fruits of their labor." I knew I needed some measurable accomplishment to have any credibility.

I knew I would only overcome my past by patience and perseverance. I could not change yesterday, but I could apply the lessons of all of my yesterdays to all of my todays and tomorrows.

Some people wander in all directions with their lives laced in confusion, when it is all so simple; Jesus said, "Follow me"— those two words answer all of our questions.

One evening late in November of 1992, just after I got up from praying, while I was sitting at the edge of my bed, I got a glimpse of evil. It happened so quickly that I could not even suggest a time frame. For some reason I had seen the depth, the depravity, and the power of evil. It scared me very badly at first. It came as such a shock, beyond what I had ever considered the reality of life. It appeared to me that the only thing preventing evil from totally overcoming man was this awesome power of God. I understood ***He is our only salvation!*** That experience scared me so much that I was filled with the need to get closer to God, the only one standing between me and that evil.

On December 1, the first anniversary of my prayer to God that changed my life, I was in prayer with my hands stretched out above me and I felt a breeze go across my hands. It continued during the rest of the time I was in prayer. I was covered with goose bumps and felt a very strong presence was with me. Later, when I talked to Ed about this experience, he mentioned references in the Bible where the Holy Spirit "moved like the wind." I was beginning to accept the idea that we cannot see all that exists. The fact that something may be difficult to believe does not make it any less true.

With these revelations, my confidence in so-called "concrete reality" became very weak. I had placed too many limitations on my belief system. It seemed God was lifting the fog so that I could see the truth. My sense of reality was changing at an incredibly rapid rate. I knew the best thing for me to do was to "go with the flow." If I tried to move against it, I sensed it immediately. I received thoughts very quickly and very clearly. If I listened, if I could still my mind, I would then receive guidance. One of my favorite Bible verses says "Be still and know that I am God."

I will never forget an evening early in December. I had been lying in bed reading and decided it was time to go to sleep. I always got down in prayer before I went to sleep. This winter evening was very cold and my apartment was a little chilly. I began making excuses to myself thinking I would get pretty cold if I got out from under the covers. In that moment I realized that the sincerity of my faith was being tested. So I got out of bed to pray. I hadn't even finished making the sign of the cross when I was filled with heat, as though a heating blanket had been turned on inside me. I couldn't help myself from bursting out in laughter at the dramatic way God had rewarded my act of faith. I prayed with a big smile on my face, filled with the joy of God's presence and with the knowledge that He was real and loved me, and I could feel that love.

Christmas of 1992 was a very pleasant time. I spent Christmas Eve with my family, who would generally stay up late and talk about events in their lives. I left my mother's home, where everyone generally gathers on the holidays (except my father), and drove to midnight Mass. I have always been uncomfortable around groups of people, so this was not an easy thing for me to do. I had been going to church several times a week but only when there weren't too many people around.

This year, I found a midnight Mass. It was beautiful. I especially enjoyed the choir singing Christmas carols. It seemed like forever since I had heard them sung. This time, they took on a special meaning for me. So much seemed new.

I could not go back and join my family after church. I was filled with gratitude for God, and I wanted to hold on to that feeling. Instead, I went back to my apartment and prayed and celebrated Christmas the way I thought it should be celebrated. I had just completed the only full year of happiness I had ever had in my life. What I had inside me was not limited to happiness—I was filled with absolute joy. I could not express it in words. It would be like trying to describe a sunset to a blind person who had never seen one.

I welcomed the new year of 1993 with enthusiasm. For the first time in my life, I was filled with hope and expectation. I anticipated each day wondering what God would reveal to me next. I had gotten into the habit of praying much of the time I spent driving late at night for the delivery company I worked for. My mind was being flooded with beauty, revelations, and spiritual growth.

January 5th was the anniversary of the day I had received a special revelation from God. I had noticed throughout my entire experience that when and if I tried to anticipate something supernatural, nothing would happen. These experiences came only in moments when I had completely abandoned myself to God, not when my thoughts were on myself. As I prayed that night, I saw hundreds of crucifixes floating toward me with cascading flowers surrounding each one. The crucifixes appeared to be made from dark wood; I could see the texture of the wood. The flowers were fashioned in such a way as to complement one another. I was drawn from the beauty of the first flower to the second. I tried to continue in my prayers, but the visions were so distracting it was hard to stay focused on prayer. It was sort of like watching the fireworks where you can hear the "ooh's" and "ah's" from the crowd. With each new burst of color your attention is drawn more and more into the beauty and excitement. I was filled with wonder as I lay there that night before sleep set in.

All is the wisdom of love.

When the transition in my life

started the year before, the thought had occurred to me that I might lose my enthusiasm. I had seen momentary enthusiasm in many people growing up. One minute they had been "Jesus freaks," the next time I would see them they were back to "normal." I did not want to be embarrassed by my visions. I didn't want to look like a fool. But as this growth continued, I became more convinced of the reality of my experiences. Whenever I felt my faith cooling, I would have another supernatural experience to keep me moving in the right direction, to keep me focused.

Late in January of 1993, I began receiving "epigrams." The material came out as complete thoughts. I would usually receive them in the evening, but also at other times of the day. The epigrams came so quickly that sometimes I could not keep up as I was trying to write everything down. I have literally hundreds of scraps of paper filled with beautiful thoughts of truth that I haven't even had time to type and organize.

I received many of these epigrams in prayer. At first I would feel guilty if I stopped praying to write something down before I forgot it, but as time went on, I realized their value, and looked at them as another of God's gifts to me. It was just as if someone was shooting pre-formed thoughts right into my mind.

> It is *only* through our acceptance of the spirit we are given access to it.

The thoughts are filled with wisdom and love, but I cannot take any credit. These thoughts are not my usual pattern of thinking; I merely write down what I receive. I am not aware of these truths until I have written them down, and only afterwards do I perceive their truth

In the second week of February, I had four days off from work. I spent much of this time reading and praying. Since I drove

Portion of Sistine Chapel (by Michelangelo, 1508-10) I saw in the clouds.

nights, I was in the habit of staying up nights and sleeping during the days. At about 4 a.m. on a Sunday morning, I had been writing and I decided to take a break and get up to stretch. I was looking out at the night sky, just day-dreaming about God and feeling very much at peace. The clouds hung low that night reflecting the light of the city, and suddenly I saw a figure in the clouds reaching out with his finger to touch something. I recognized it as a picture from Michelangelo's painting on the ceiling of the Sistine Chapel. This was a perfect image, absolutely identifiable and perfectly clear. I had a book filled with famous paintings, so I started paging through it, to find out who this person was. I thought it could be very relevant in light of my other experiences. I thought it might be a saint or some Biblical person. I located the picture and I was amazed to find it was Michelangelo's image of God breathing life into Adam. It was not a saint; I had seen a vision of God. This cloud formation was so clear and detailed. Anyone who saw it and had seen pictures of the Sistine Chapel would recognize the figure immediately. It lasted only for a few moments before it blended with the other clouds, but I was sure that I was meant to see it at that particular moment. Once again my faith was strengthened.

March was a month of deepening prayer. I could sense the growth that was going on. I still struggled very hard to put my new attitude into practice. I had always been very impatient, very critical of others, extremely selfish, and arrogant, and these flaws in my personality were not easily changed. I would try to treat people better and to demonstrate kindness, but sometimes my ego would sneak in and lure me into my old responses.

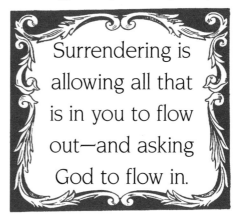

Surrendering is allowing all that is in you to flow out—and asking God to flow in.

Many times I went home thinking I should have handled a situation differently. I often found myself disappointed in my progress. But I decided to continue doing my best and trust God to help me become a better person. This was the sixteenth month of my new life, and although my progress seemed minimal, I still could recognize it. It took time to become a healthy human being after spending most of my life headed in the wrong direction. While alive, we can never become completely perfect, but we need to stay on that pathway. When our physical body dies, God will bring us the rest of the way home. 🌾

It is only necessary to love
to acquire wisdom;
for true wisdom is born of true love,
as true love is born of true wisdom.

19

Who would choose to be a pebble in a river, when they can truly become the river itself?

URING APRIL, 1993, I LOST MY JOB. I had not anticipated this event. I liked that job a lot, especially the fact that I got out at night when there were not too many people around. I had a chance to focus on what I felt was important in my life, prayer.

I started collecting unemployment, but it just was not quite enough money to make ends meet. Occasionally I would get small jobs to make a little extra money so that I could at least cover my basic needs. I decided that since I had free time, I would begin writing this book. I began it, finishing about half of it before I started receiving epigrams again.

I was deluged with them. I took their appearance to mean I should not concentrate just on my book, but also on doing something with them to earn enough money to continue the book. I sent some of my material to some of the larger publishing houses, thinking they were my best bet because of the volume of material they print each year. I received several rejections; and in talking to people I learned that some of the larger publishers did not even read unsolicited material. They had plenty of material and were taking less and less risks with new authors.

I was somewhat discouraged, but I understood I was not to do things my way anymore; I was to trust God. So, I continued writing and occasionally submitting material to publishers, trusting God with my future. It was a little hard to do sometimes because I had no skills other than writing. I had only two years of college, which was not enough to get in the door of most places, and my work record showed the unreliability that goes along with thirty years of addiction to drugs and alcohol. As far as personal references, no one wanted to vouch for me with the kind of background I had. I had been totally undependable all my life, and no one knew of the changes that were taking place inside me. I had told a few people, but no one seemed to believe me so I stopped telling others, except Ed.

> ## AA Step 5
> We admitted to God, to ourselves, and to another human being the exact nature of our wrongs.

I did talk to some of my family and some people I knew to be Christians. It saddened me that I could not convey to others what God was doing in my life. It saddened me that I had destroyed all my credibility by the way I had lived my life. I realized that my life was changing, but I wanted people to know *now* that God was real. It couldn't help but change the world.

I began getting involved in photography. I wanted pictures to tie together with the epigrams, to make a more effective presentation. I spent most of June and July writing and taking pictures. It was just as if God gave me some time off not only to grow, but to enjoy myself and enjoy the beauty all around me.

I did not have enough experience to take pictures well, and I ended up wasting about half of my film because the shots were not just right. I approached the College of Saint Benedict in St. Joseph, Minnesota, hoping to get some help from them with photography. I knew they had access to many very beautiful pictures, so I asked them for permission to pair their works with mine. I met with Mariterese Woida, O.S.B., and Thomasette Scheeler, O.S.B., both of St. Joseph, Minnesota, who asked to see the material I had written. I explained to them how I had gotten the material, and they were impressed enough by what they saw to agree to give me access to their pictures. It was nice to get such a vote of confidence from the Sisters.

I was able to come up with some very beautiful combinations using the photographs from Saint Benedict's with the epigrams. The idea of using this material for spiritual greeting cards came to me. There was nothing quite like what I had on the market at that time. There were a lot of flowery cards, but I thought I could gear my material to the younger generation. They needed something to connect with, some way of dealing with God comfortably. My material approached God in a spiritual, non-threatening way. Young people did not use the word "God" much, but it was very acceptable to talk about spiritual things. Spiritual books and songs have become very popular among the younger people. It is OK to be spiritual! I felt my cards would meet a need that was out there for younger people to express their spirituality with pride and sincerity, and feel comfortable when doing so.

I sent some samples of the cards to some greeting card companies, but I only received form letters rejecting my material.

I admit it was somewhat disheartening. I was learning, however, how to accept rejection without resentment. Nothing happened to me that did not provide an opportunity to grow both spiritually and emotionally.

> Love is the fabric of our beings,
> woven together
> by the angels of God.

In the middle of August, I began reciting the Rosary each evening before bed. It was very difficult for me because of my lack of self-discipline, but I knew it would be good for me for several reasons. But foremost, I felt compelled by the Spirit of God. I did not know much about the Rosary, so I began reading different books and articles from Christian magazines so that I might understand the meaning and purpose behind the recitation. After I had been reciting it for about a week, I read that we could ask Mary for special graces if we recited the Rosary regularly. I thought about what graces I needed most in my life, and I felt that I needed patience and tolerance more than anything else. So I began asking for those graces when I had finished my prayers in the evening. It was about a week later, when I was just getting down to pray, a thought shot into my head so quickly I could not ignore it. I did not need to ask for "patience and tolerance;" what I needed was "humility." It did not make sense to me immediately, but after I had thought about it for a little while, it made perfect sense. If I could become humble, I would automatically become more patient and tolerant of others. God's touch revealed not only my significance, but my insignificance as well.

> AA STEP 6
> We were entirely ready to have God remove all these defects of character.

I had heard about Rosary chains changing to a beautiful gold color at Medjugorje, Yugoslavia, and I thought how beautiful it would be if a transformation would happen to my Rosary, even though it was an inexpensive one with a stainless steel chain and plastic beads. I wished I had a beautiful glass Rosary if it were going to change colors. But then almost immediately, I realized the error of my thinking. The Rosary's value is not in the material, but the spiritual. I saw then where my own arrogance would take me if I allowed. I knew it had been the ego's thought, but I received the spiritual answer because I listened.

About a week later, I removed the medals I wore around my neck, not something I commonly do. I have one particular medal that has the face of Jesus on it. It is made out of sterling silver, but I noticed that it had changed. It had turned a beautiful rose color. Once again, my faith was strengthened. I shared my gratitude with God.

I still battled with my old behaviors and reactions. It was at this time that I saw the power of the "ego." The ego is basically and potentially good; but we in our own ignorance, without guidance from God, use it wrongly, selfishly, *humanly*. We take the attitude that we do not require help or guidance, thereby allowing our pride to dictate our attitude, our decisions, and our behavior. We live our lives on the assumption that we have all the answers, and we do not need God's help. But God's guidance converts the ego's selfishness into love. We must get on the correct path if we ever hope to arrive at our destination.

The ego's negative power had run my life, and a change of leadership would mean "wars" inside of me. In self-examination, I broke myself down into four categories: first, the Spirit of God that was within me; second, the ego (myself, my will, my energy, that part of me that is susceptible to evil); third, that serious part of myself, the part that was analytical and critical; and fourth, what I like to call "the fun guy," that part of me that looks at things with a sense of humor. I have listed these four traits in the order of the power I felt they held. By dividing my behavior into categories of "personalities," I was then able to isolate and recognize where my response came from and what its motivation was. Then I began to see very quickly where good and evil were. And my choices would determine where I stayed, with good or evil.

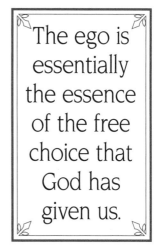

The ego is essentially the essence of the free choice that God has given us.

Judging from my experiences, goodness is far more powerful than evil. I saw that the Spirit of God quieted and stilled my selfishness and my pride, and re-directed my energy long enough for me to look for the value in a decision I was about to make. I discovered I did have a choice, and I did not always have to yield to the ego's negative power.

I watched the ego create conflict after conflict in myself and others. I saw that it was a continuous battle. If I were not very watchful and careful, I would be swept up in the ego's grab for glory, prominence, and control. I saw how I had allowed the ego's negative energy to control my entire life. I was proud, boastful, aggressive, selfish, vain, and lazy. The ego's negative energy tries to interrupt people, not to listen, to find ways to use people. It places its own importance above all things. The ego is what carries grudges; the ego is the thing that creates doubts; the ego holds the potential evil in us all.

As I watched my behavior and my responses, I saw how Satan plans and works to win this dangerous game. These words came to me in a flood, just rushing into my consciousness: "Look, here's what we'll do: we'll get their attention focused on anything other than God. We'll scramble their brains with earthly pleasures; we'll get them so caught up in the pursuit of these pleasures, they will not even care about a future, just themselves…the future be damned! Live for the moment! God and the day after tomorrow will be the last thing on their minds; it will be an alien thought. They won't even have time to think about others—let alone God."

I began to be able to catch the ego's attempt to continue operating within me in a negative way. The more I watched the ego's operation, the more subtle and sneaky it became. It had had its way with me all my life, controlling everything, and it was not going to relinquish its power without a struggle. So struggle we did.

In the middle of September, about two weeks after I received the information on the ego, I was given the word "forgiveness." I became aware of the ego's part in the process of holding grudges. The ego built the walls that will not allow forgiveness to enter our lives. The Spirit of God dissolves those walls, if we ask, and if we allow.

Free choice gives us the opportunity to determine our priorities. Once we determine them, we are set upon our path. If we choose to become forgiving, we see that ignorance is to blame for error. Thus we should forgive the acts of others done in ignorance. If we are unable to forgive, we are unable to proceed in our own growth. We are held back by our bitterness. Bitterness is like a little angry person who moves into our soul, and raises so much hell that our thinking is distorted. With him inside, we blame everyone else for our own misery. It is far better to fill our consciousness with God's soothing love than to allow petty demons to cause constant turmoil in our lives.

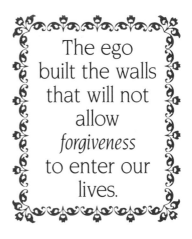

The ego built the walls that will not allow *forgiveness* to enter our lives.

God's love leads us to acceptance, acknowledgment and action. We must illustrate the beauty of God in our actions. In prayer, we give ourselves to God; in action, we pledge our allegiance to God.

Being a representative of Christ is a challenging responsibility. We have a different perspective when we are responsible to God. Sometimes God gives us things to do that are not on our list. Where someone else may find it difficult to forgive, that is our opportunity to demonstrate our faith in God, to live it. The basis of any sound religion is love. In demonstrating our faith through love, we are making it easier for others to reciprocate.

God gave us an imagination so that we could perform goodness with spontaneity. The only magic I know of is love. As we love, so are we loved in return. We must put our resentment and anger aside if we wish to participate in the plans of God, because they simply do not belong in the process. They are weeds in God's garden.

About two weeks later, I got another word that I was to learn about, "truth." We have tried to adapt God's principles to our own advantage, but the process does not work that way. The main thing that keeps us from moving forward in our lives is our refusal to alter our lives as a result of knowing the truth about how we live. For the most part, we choose to abide by the commandments of God only so long as they suit our needs. Such limited

> We have tried
> to adapt God's
> principles to
> our own
> advantage.
> The process
> does not work
> that way.

"convenience" allows evil to enter our lives. And with the operation of the ego, selfishness is rampant and we tend to justify whatever we want to do. We make excuses; we somehow rationalize that the rules were made for others, not ourselves; we refuse to accept the truth; we have more urgent things to do. It is not so much that truth is unavailable to us, as that we just do not want to hear it.

Our arrogance is the shovel we use for digging a deeper hell for ourselves. We are, for the most part, selfish, greedy, and miserly. There is plenty of food for everyone in this world—yet there are thousands of people dying daily from starvation! We have enough medicine to help hundreds of thousands of people—but thousands are dying daily from disease. We spend billions of dollars annually on military weapons to kill people—rather than investing it in humanitarian projects. As I view the faces of the dying children that cross our airways and are in our newspapers and magazines daily, I cannot help but feel ashamed for being part of the problem which allowed these things to occur. I ask myself what right I have to live in a society that is overflowing with an abundance of food, medicine and essential goods, yet I watch the faces of hunger and poverty daily on news broadcasts. God told us to "love our neighbor as ourselves," but for the most part, we ignore our neighbors and love ourselves.

In mid-October, I received another word: "fear." While driving over to Ed's house, in a space of less than a city block, I saw the havoc fear raises in our lives. Fear prevents us from making wise decisions which will improve our lives. Fear actually encourages negative, irrational behavior. We are afraid of what someone might think or say about us. We are afraid to get close to others. We are afraid to say "I love you." We are afraid of illness, the dark, poverty, handicapped and different persons, and new ideas. But most of all, we are *afraid of change*. If we give in to that last fear, then nothing in our lives can get better. Resistance to change freezes us to the spot we are in at that moment. If we want new results that are *different* from the old results, then we must do things *differently* than we have in the past. To make that change we must face our fear with courage, faith, and resolve.

One of the reasons we have such a hard time finding God is because we cannot get off the beaten path. All of that can change. We must remember it is through God's mercy that we have only pencilled in our pathway; we have not used indelible ink! Thus, God's bountiful forgiveness can actually erase our detours and deadends and make straight the route. Unfortunately, many people would rather flounder than admit they need the help of God.

> Our *fear* is manifest by evil; give it that kind of credibility.

Life on earth is one obstacle after another; the purpose is spiritual growth. At the end of each day, if we have lived it correctly, we should be more able to cope with the obstacles placed along our pathway to God. These obstacles can help us to grow, if viewed in the right perspective.

During the first few days of November, my attention was drawn to the word "authority." I have had a great deal of difficulty in my life accepting the orders of others. I had been in constant rebellion against authority figures all my life. I began to see how submitting to another's orders was a manner of humbling myself. And I recognized humility as being a quality that God wanted in me. I also recognized the importance of remaining humble under the leadership of others. One should respect those in authority if they use their authority in gentle, kind, and loving ways. While our leaders may not be perfect for the job, and it may even seem at times that we may be more knowledgeable about the particular situation we are dealing with, it is still our responsibility to respond with obedience. The lessons we learn in that process allow growth to take place in our lives.

> Authority is a gift we are given; we should treat it accordingly.

God's laws are not always compatible with our desires. They reveal the value of obedience. We must practice obedience to God's laws in our lives; only in that way are we able to move closer to Him.

It is an altogether different matter if an authority figure tells us to do something *contrary* to God's laws. Then we have the right to question the person's authority. But effective and righteous authority must be tempered with humility; and in turn, we must respect and obey those who have been put into a position of authority.

It was a very smooth transition from "authority" to the importance of our "attitude" in our daily lives. Our attitude can prevent us from loving or being loved, preventing us from establishing healthy relationships. Our attitude very often determines if we will get a particular job. Our attitude is something we pass on to our children. It becomes our legacy when we are gone. Our attitude is the thing that keeps us from God, or can bring us closer to Him. Others can easily affect our attitude, if we allow it. So, before anything else can change, we must change our attitude.

We must change our priorities, because our attitude is a reflection of them. When God says our priority should be love, if we value anything higher, we will find ourselves lost and stumbling. "Love thy neighbor as thyself" is the way God's law reads. There is nothing complicated about it; it is very clear. Above all else we should love.

I do not see love as the primary motivator in people's lives. This neglect is terribly unfortunate because we have such joy available to us simply by surrendering to God. We have such arrogance that we find it difficult to admit we are not in total control. Your attitude will determine if the door to God is open or closed. It is that simple.

The next word that was called to my attention was "perseverance." Once again I could see how that concept was tied to my attitude. Earlier in this book, I said many people had told me they had "tried" God, but it just did not work. Faith in God is not something we "try on," like a new jacket or blouse; faith is something we *do!* Faith means we must move forward in spite of doubt. Sticking to the pathway is perseverance. To say we are merely going to try, implies that we might not succeed. If we have such an attitude, why bother starting out on the journey at all? We must persevere in the face of doubt, and God will reward us for our perseverance with tremendous help.

I "tried" God many times, but never with total commitment. My life deteriorated, in spite of my own feeble efforts at improvement. When I approached God with conviction, I knew that I had no answers for my problems. Through my sincerity God lifted me up. For every little bit of faith in God, He gave me, in return, massive amounts of love and understanding.

I am very thankful I persevered because my life changed substantially—more than I could have imagined in my wildest dreams. I was a lonely, lost man, with my fists clenched in anger. When I reached out to God, He gently loosened my grip, then filled my heart with His love. Our love for God must be our priority if we desire goodness in our lives. As a result of our perseverance, God dramatically encourages spiritual growth, very beautifully.

First, God fills us with

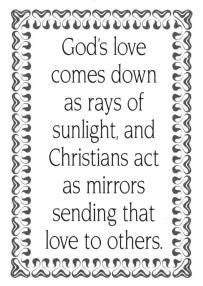

God's love comes down as rays of sunlight, and Christians act as mirrors sending that love to others.

His love, and then that love is radiated outward to others. Once we experience God's love, we will spend the rest of our lives thanking Him. And we will find that how much we trust and love God determines how much help we will receive from Him.

It used to make me uncomfortable hearing people say they loved God and Jesus so much. I couldn't understand the power of the love they felt, so I foolishly chalked it off as wishful thinking on the part of others. Then God revealed Himself to me...and I understood: this is love you have never experienced with your parents, your spouse, your child, or any other person or thing in life. There is power I cannot put into words held within this love.

Our true value is only realized through our union with God. This union is reached through faith, trust, and perseverance.

20 Love is longing made whole.

ECEMBER 1, 1993, WAS THE SECOND anniversary of my new life. I remember at that time looking back in amazement at the changes in my attitude and the path my life was taking. I remembered how I had wondered in the beginning if I would lose enthusiasm for my new beliefs. It was just the opposite! It was as though I was becoming obsessed with God and the spiritual realm. God drew my trust from myself to Himself. My life had never held such hope.

As the days had passed, I could feel new growth happening each and every day. I would look back at the day before and realize that I was actually happier, more joyful, with each new day. I did not sense this joy only occasionally. I sensed it every single day. I had benefited from my experiences, and I understood more about why we are here and what is the purpose of our lives.

It was on this evening of December first that I received a glimpse of the intense joy that awaited us all through the recognition and realization of God. For the briefest moment I was allowed access to heaven. I felt the intensity of that love for just a moment, but it will always be in my memory. I have nothing to compare this experience to except when I had been given that very brief but intense look into the evil that exists here on earth. They were such intense opposites.

In that first week of December, I received another word, "judgment." My judgment of others had been very harsh all my life, as had the judgments I made about myself. I thought I was brutally honest in my judgment. I would have been very effective as a critic. I didn't "cut anyone any slack." But I realized through the recognition of my own errors how wrong I had been about everything. I have no right to condemn the actions of others, having been in the midst of ignorance most of my life. I did not feel worthy of judging others, and I also saw how wrong I had been in my judgment of others.

God said, very clearly, we should love our neighbor—not just the one whose yard is trimmed and filled with gardens and flowers, but also the neighbor's whose yard is filled with debris piling higher and higher. We can never know the particular circumstances of another person's life. We are not in a position to pick and choose whom to love and when we will love them; that kind of thinking is not of God. It is very likely that someone who we may assume is very ignorant is aware of many answers that trouble us all. Do not be so quick to judge such a person by his appearance, or his speech, or his lack of "pertinent" knowledge. Who would have guessed we would have ever found the beautiful pearl that is at the heart of an oyster—surrounded by a rough exterior we call its shell? There is much more value at the heart of a thing, than on the exterior.

AA Step 7
We humbly asked Him to remove our shortcomings.

I also realized that if I wanted forgiveness, I must learn how to forgive others for their errors. I saw that love and forgiveness were reciprocal. It is something which is unavailable to us until we are ready to love and forgive others for their errors.

It is extremely easy to judge others. A friend of mine made a judgment about someone else, but called it an "observation," not a judgment. There is an extremely fine line between the two because of the ego. An "observation" is supposedly objective without the responsibility or "satisfaction" of passing judgment. We love to judge others because by pointing out their deficiencies, we cover our own. Thus, if we allow pride to participate in our observation, it is no longer objective, no longer an observation, but now becomes a judgment.

Our ego's negative force believes it is always right in its condemnation of others. It is the master of deception, not unlike Satan.

I believe the Spirit of God resides in our conscience once we ask God into our lives. My conscience tells me I have no right to judge others. I listen and obey my conscience as much as I am capable of now. I pray that someday I will be able to resist all sin and temptation. I do not, however, expect that to happen while I am here on earth. We can only do our best and pray that our best will become God's will for us. We should remember, we shall be judged in the same manner as we judge others.

The words *mercy* and *love* have a great deal in common.

Christmas was fast approaching when I received the word "mercy." I thought about how appropriate that was at this time of the year. It has been said by our Holy Mother in Her apparitions at Medju- gorje that Christmas was the time that the most people were released from purgatory and wel- comed into heaven, Mary called it "a great time of grace." I had no difficulty believing that observation, since my journey to God had begun on December 1, 1991.

I was on my knees in prayer to God when I asked Him why these things were happening to me. I told Him I did not deserve them, especially after all the terrible things I had done in my life. With absolutely no hesitation I received this thought, "You would never have done those things had you known me." In that instant I realized the truth in that statement. I would have led my life much differently if I had known God was real. There was no question about that. I realized that all my troubles occurred out of ignorance—ignorance about the reality of God. I saw that ignorance is not something to be ashamed of, it just means I did not have enough information to make the right decisions. With that understanding, I was beginning to release the guilt and shame I had carried around for years because of my behavior. I understood and accepted the responsibilities that went with my behavior. I had suffered the consequences of my actions. They could change now if it was something I desired. Without question, it was my desire.

I felt drawn more toward God then than I had ever been. I longed to be closer and closer. My life had held so much emptiness. I was like a man who was dying of thirst who suddenly came upon a well. I never wanted to be thirsty again. I had no intention of leaving that well; it was my life.

If God could be that merciful with me, I could not begrudge anyone else that same degree of forgiveness. Those are the rules; that is the reality of God.

AA Steps 8 & 9
We made a list of all persons we had harmed, and became willing to make amends to them all.
We made direct amends to such people wherever possible, except when to do so would injure them or others.

By the time Christmas of 1993 arrived, I had received a great deal of insight. In looking back, I could see how wrong I had been throughout my entire life, and I had thought so highly of myself intellectually. It was easy to see I had a great deal to learn. I wondered why it had taken 43 years for me to recognize the truth. I wondered how I could have thought I had all the answers when everything around me was tumbling down. It had taken me that long to realize the debris that I lived in was my own arrogance.

It was extremely humbling to suddenly realize that I had been wrong about so much. But God, in His mercy, gave me a second chance, a new opportunity to get it right. I wanted to, in some way, repair all the damage I had done in my life. I believe very strongly there is a reason for everything that has happened to me. I have been guided and coaxed. It seemed that if I strayed from my path out of ignorance and arrogance, I was gently helped back on that path with the sudden realization of my error. I no longer considered myself in control of my life. I had turned everything over to God. He was doing a far better job with me than I had done. I was His piece of clay, and I was loving every minute of my molding in His hands.

> AA STEP 10
> We continued to take personal inventory and when we were wrong promptly admitted it.

On December 28, 1993, I knelt in prayer, and the only light in the room came from a single candle. When I had completed my prayers, I blew out the candle. I thought what a beautiful thing it would be if the candle's flame would light just as a little sign from God. Immediately, though, I saw the error. I was asking God for more proof. I realized how selfish it was and I apologized for my lack of faith. In that instant I heard what sounded like a pop, a very small burst of energy. It was similar to the sound I had heard when I was holding the crucifix in prayer when it began to crackle with the sound of static electricity and the crucifix got very hot. It was a similar sound, but louder. I opened my eyes and lifted my head. The candle was now lighted and burning brightly on my little altar.

At that time, I took it as matter of fact. I just smiled and thanked God. But when I told Ed about it, he thought it was a pretty dramatic sign. He thought it was a powerful piece of evidence, and I should be thankful. The more I thought about it, the more I realized how right Ed was. I was dealing with mighty powerful energy, and very few people ever have similar experiences to mine. I was very grateful. I still battled with the question, why was this happening to me, but I did not allow it to stop my pursuit.

I was not to be disappointed. On December 29th, while reciting the Rosary, I began to have visions that were absolutely beautiful. They were much like the visions of crucifixes and flowers I had seen before. There were many crucifixes floating toward me from the distance; this time they were made of jewels, almost diamond-like, and were surrounded and wrapped in gorgeous flowers that were filled with beautiful, almost-fluorescent colors, extremely bright. The whole vision was one of cascading flowers wrapped around and draped over the crucifixes. I have never seen anything as beautiful as this splendid vision, ever in my life. I was overwhelmed by the beauty I was seeing.

When I was in prayer, I was aware of a constant presence of only what can be described as love. It felt as though I had suddenly been enveloped in a warm cloud, but in spite of the warmth, my body was always covered with goose bumps. When it first began to happen, I was always amazed; but I grew used to it and I did not consider it unusual anymore. On the contrary, if I did not sense this presence when I got down in prayer, I waited until this presence moved over me and engulfed me to begin praying. It was as if I had to wait for someone else to arrive before anything else could be done. Now, I believe that presence to be the Spirit of God. And I believe that Spirit of God is escorted by the angels of Heaven.

> God takes frantic enthusiasm and transforms it into a steady beam of light.

The Gift

Give me words, my Lord,

That I might give them to others.

Give me dreams, my Lord,

that I might find You

in the midst of them.

Give me hope, my Lord,

for in that moment,

I am Yours.

We should allow the Spirit of God to seize the opportunity to work in us, which, at times, may require patience. But our reward for faith, trust, and patience, is grace from God. If we demonstrate confidence in the reality of God, He will give us proof of His love in our lives. As it is written, "Act as if I were, and thou shall know that I AM."

I spent New Year's Eve very quietly. But in looking back through my life, I remembered how important the occasion had seemed, a time to "celebrate" by getting drunk and high. That priority had changed. I longed for the peace I felt when I was in contemplative prayer. I loved the solitude of my small apartment, surrounded by plants, with soft beautiful music playing. In the evening I would light candles and I just seemed to float through what God was giving me.

On Sunday, January 2, 1994, I was praying the Rosary in the evening when suddenly the darkness I was seeing (with my eyes closed) changed. What I was seeing went from darkness to a solid beige. Then it appeared that I was in the galaxy moving forward at a tremendous speed. I could see stars and planets as I moved forward, quickly leaving them behind. I saw a phosphorous blue planet with a matching blue atmosphere around it. It was as if I were on a flight through an unfolding, ever-changing universe. Nothing was stationary; everything seemed to flow from its center outward. It was as if life or existence were a process of perpetual motion. It gave me the feeling of being insignificant when I saw the majesty of what I was "passing through."

I found it very difficult to concentrate on the prayers I was saying. I was continually distracted by my visions. There were several times I opened my eyes to try to concentrate more fully on my prayers, but as soon as I closed my eyes, I was immediately swept up in the vision again. I felt like I was seeing the enormity of the "real" world and the complexity of its existence. I also felt very strongly that the human mind could not analyze my visions. I felt that things were being put into perspective for me.

The following Sunday, January 9, 1994, I was once again reciting the Rosary. I was meditating on the nativity of Jesus, when

I began to see floating crucifixes wrapped in small pink roses. Then an archway appeared that was formed by hundreds of colorful flowers. As I passed through this archway, I saw the baby Jesus lying in a cradle of flowers. The entire cradle looked as if it was made of beautiful flowers interwoven with one another. Nowhere had I seen such beauty, not in photos or paintings.

During this time, I generally took whatever I could find in the way of work during the winter months. The rest of the year I would paint houses and make minor repairs to homes. This kind of work had allowed me to be my own boss for the most part. I had no other skills which would allow me to make enough money to live on. I was especially effective working with delinquent children, but the wages paid for that type of work were just not enough to make ends meet.

I began driving a taxi several days a week. I enjoyed driving a taxi. I met and dealt with a wide variety of people. It was the perfect job for me to begin to use a lot of the knowledge I had received. There were challenges and obstacles to overcome each and every day. I saw how important my attitude was in dealing with others. I began to have some flexibility that I had not had before. Instead of being the wind, I was becoming a leaf in the wind. I stepped back and listened; I had given God control of my life. I knew I would be a fool if I allowed the ego's negative forces once again to run my life. Now I asked God to solve any problems that might come up, and He never disappointed me.

In my daily routine as a taxi driver, I dealt with many handicapped people. I came to recognize an innocence those people seemed to hold, a sweetness unspoiled by mankind. Some of the more severely handicapped people could not speak, but they sure could smile. Within those smiles, I saw the goodness of God. To me,

> The measurements of God are not external but internal.

there seemed to be a lot of uncharted territory within these people. The more I worked with them, the more I saw that their handicaps were not very important. It was what they had in their hearts that gave them value. They had hope; they had courage; they accepted their hardships without bitterness. I could learn a lot from them if I did not make the mistake of thinking I was in some way better than they were. When we think we are better than others, what we are doing is building a wall—a wall that keeps revelation out, and emptiness in.

I remember one fellow in particular. He could not talk, and he didn't seem to have much control over his muscles. He needed my help getting in the taxi as well as getting to his door once I got him home. He always had a smile for me. Sometimes he'd reach out and put his arm around me and give me a big hug. It seemed like he knew I was "safe." I was not going to reject him. He lived life as fully as he could within his limitations. He always seemed enthusiastic and happy. In the beginning I felt uneasy getting too close to him because I would feel embarrassed by his handicap. As time went by, that uneasiness was replaced by compassion for him. I found myself feeling fortunate for the opportunity to experience the lessons he could teach me. It was not necessary for him to speak for me to learn from him. He demonstrated qualities many of us never attain. His patience, his perseverance, his joy, and his love for others came through very clearly to me. What allowed all of those things to be expressed by him was his attitude.

Emulate Christ; dwell on truth;
live to love; give to gain;
lie down that you may be
lifted up.

21

What we have heard is true; it is all done with mirrors; love is the reflection of Christ.

N JANUARY 25, 1994, I WAS AGAIN IN prayer when I had a vision of Jesus sitting on a throne with bright light coming from the base of the throne. Then I saw someone approaching the throne. As this person moved toward Jesus, I saw Jesus stand up and move forward in front of the throne. As He did so, I saw the light was not coming from the base of the throne, but from Jesus Himself. It appeared as though Jesus blessed this person who approached Him, and then the vision ended.

Visions of crucifixes shrouded in flowers were an almost ever-present companion when I was reciting the Rosary during this time. I found myself accepting these things as part of my prayer life. They no longer distracted me nearly as much as they had initially. What struck me was the extraordinary beauty of everything I saw. The visions were showing me things that were not man-made. The designs were so intricate and beautiful, man did not seem capable of creating them. I was fascinated by them.

There were times when I would try to explain my visions to Ed, but I did not feel I could do justice to the beauty I had witnessed. The visions were occurring with such frequency and changing rapidly, that I was drawn further into their beauty. It was difficult for me to observe them and then repeat them in sequence to anyone. I could only attempt a description, but I knew it always fell short of describing their incredible beauty. The crucifixes appeared to be made from wood, diamond, or crystal. Some seemed to be made of thousands of colorful jewels. The flowers which surrounded and clung to the crucifixes were most often roses. Although I would begin to see a vision from the exterior, it was as though I then moved right through one vision to another.

I continued driving a taxi into the month of February, then business slowed down significantly because of the warmer weather approaching. I had to look for an income that would be more consistent. I found a job assembling metal beams to hold metal shelving for merchandise in a large, newly built, retail store. The second day on the job, I injured my back while lifting some beams above my head to another person. This injury was very discouraging for me. It was bad enough I had to seek out work no one else really wanted because of my lack of experience and my poor work history, but now I couldn't even do simple work because of the pain.

"Love" is only a synonym for "God."

Tests revealed disc degeneration and a bulging disc. I became very concerned about what I would be able to do in the future. I was afraid I was going to be severely limited in my choices. It was at this time I was drawn back to writing, the only thing I could do without pain.

Throughout the month of March, I continued to "receive" epigrams which I put down on paper. In April, these epigrams seemed to change from single lines into small paragraphs or poems filled with truth. At times, I would receive an entire poem in a matter of minutes. Here is one of the poems I received:

The Pearl

Now,
unbridled,
I run through the green fields,
experiencing my innocence
for the first time.

What hell I came from,
what misadventure,
looking, always looking
out there for the answer.

Then when I had torn
all that God had given me,
dressed in rags
and self-pity,
when I had dug a deeper hell
than anyone was meant to dwell,
He revealed Himself to me.

He was not out there in the world,
nor did He choose to hide,
I found Him where I had never looked...
way down deep inside.

At times, it was very difficult to write the words down as
quickly as they came to me. The words came in a complete
thought or concept. It was truly amazing to read what I had written down after I had received the words. While I was receiving the
information, I could not check it for consistency. I had to wait
until afterwards, but I always found the thoughts were complete
and consistent. I knew these things were not coming from me; I
was not that wise or that capable. I was learning as I wrote down

the information. Everything I received was during contemplative prayer. It was as though if I left myself open, the Holy Spirit poured into me and filled me with knowledge I had not had access to before.

On May 13, 1994, I began spending a great deal more of my time in prayer to our Holy Mother, Mary. Immediately things began to change. I was lifted higher than I had ever been lifted before. I was filled with a sense of joy to the point of bursting. I was so excited I could barely sleep. It seemed that every single problem I had at that time, financial and personal, was solved. I was filled with peace and indescribable joy. I was flooded with visions of tremendous beauty. As soon as I closed my eyes in prayer, I saw hundreds of hearts floating out at me. In the midst of these hearts I saw one lone, inverted heart. I remember thinking how strange it was that I would see only one heart like that. No sooner did I have that thought than I saw the head of a dove begin to emerge from the heart's point and the sides of the heart turned into the wings of a dove as it flew upward in flight. The colors of the hearts ranged from pink to a deep, rich burgundy color—I was told later by Kay, Ed's wife, that was the anniversary of the day our Holy Mother appeared at Fatima for the first time.

Only once did I see Christ crucified on the cross. All of the other visions I had of crucifixes were without Christ.

I had a vision of a page of sheet music with just the outline of bells in a rich, gold color in place of the musical notes. Behind this image was a beautiful, deep, rich red color. I could hear angelic voices joined in songs of praise of God.

The intensity of these visions and others lasted for fourteen days. During this period of time, I received an impression of the importance of faith in our lives. We must move forward with confidence in spite of doubt. It is only then that we begin to understand. This is the way God begins to work in our lives; it simply is not done any other way.

I understood that we are not measured by the mistakes we make, but by the steps we take toward God. We will find that the things of true value unify themselves on our journey to God through faith and prayer. We do not just happen upon spiritual enlightenment; rather, it is given to us by God through the Holy Spirit. The Holy Spirit is our lifeline to God, and we communicate with God through the Holy Spirit when we pray. We will find that prayer opens locked doors and that when we live in anticipation of God, every moment *is* new!

"In God We Trust" should be impressed upon on our hearts and should dictate our behavior at all times. And while it is natural to question our faith in a crisis, it should also be the natural time to pray. We must remember always, we are a reflection of our faith, an example unto others.

I do not know why my experiences intensified after I began to pray the Rosary to Mary. The recitation of the Rosary seemed to encourage my emotional and spiritual growth. It was during this recitation that my visions became more frequent and my understanding of my purpose became clearer. The prayers had the effect of water poured over a dry and lifeless plant. I felt as though I was experiencing the reality of life for the first time. My thirst was being quenched, my emptiness filled. I could recognize growth as never before.

I do not feel in any way that this was a denominational experience; *it was an experience of God.* And in this process, I was shown that only a religion that encompasses the love of *all* people is sound. Denominations are merely different paths we take, paths that all ultimately lead to God. *Love does not separate, but draws together.* We are spokes in a wheel, the center of which is God.

Beginning in June, I began to "receive" longer poems, some of them as long as forty lines. I merely wrote them down as I received them. The following is one I especially like:

Lullaby of God

God comes in and touches me
and fills my sails with wind;
my path is clear, the moon is full,
I am heading home again.

There are angels in my room at night,
they are angels of the light,
I follow them in my dreams
and all throughout the night.

They are taking me away from here,
they are determined in their quest;
they have shown me parts of heaven,
and now I will see the rest.

There are gardens everywhere we go
and the air is filled with love,
promises of hopes and dreams
and angels from above.

I cannot stop these journeys,
nor would I if I could,
for God has given me this gift
and I know that it is good.

So, when I awake in the morning,
when night has turned to day,
I will tell you where I have been
but not allowed to stay.

It would be so much better
if you would come along,
for a song sung with another
is truly then a song.

There was a time I had been thinking about my relationship with my father, wondering why it had been such a struggle for both of us. And the following poem came to me:

Paths

As I grew older
and from dreams awoke,
I realized inside myself,
I was just the doll
my father broke.

Kept a distance from my heart,
hidden truths from the start,
I could not come to recognize
that emptiness within his eyes.

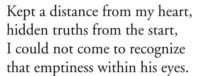

The sorrow was passed down to me,
the errors were included;
I shriveled up instead of growing,
and found myself excluded.

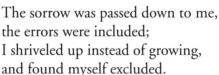

And as these truths came to me
and I had somehow grown,
I came to realize that my dad
once had a father of his own.

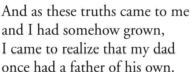

And chances are Dad hurt the same,
though I never knew he cried,
but I do recall that broken doll
the day his father died.

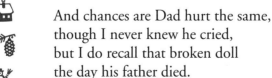

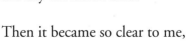

Then it became so clear to me,
that in our final destiny,
it matters not who breaks the doll,
but what we learn from it all.

My relationship with my father has improved a great deal. I believe we both recognize our mistakes and have begun to accept all of this as a growth process, as well as a gift when properly understood.

It was as though my questions were being answered as quickly as I asked them. The shadows in my life were disappearing, and I was, without question, "seeing the light." What a beautiful way to learn! The lessons came in such a beautiful way that they stayed with me, replacing those hurtful things that used to fill my life: fear, anger, loneliness, despair, and a sense of being lost without a purpose. I now recognized my purpose.

Renée Domeier, O.S.B., a friend I had become very close to, once asked me what I thought the reason was behind my receiving these visions and revelations. My reply, given after about a year of these experiences, was that I felt I was supposed to teach others. It was about a year later when I realized I was only the messenger; God shared His will with me and my purpose is to share these experiences with others.

> AA STEP 11
> We sought through prayer and meditation to improve our conscious contact with God *as we understood Him*, praying only for knowledge of His will for us and the power to carry that out.

I believe we are approaching a time of significant change. That change is becoming more and more evident daily through fulfillment of Biblical prophecy. It is time for all of us to make a decision, a decision for Christ—or a decision for evil. Making no decision is, in effect, a decision for evil, for it represents complacency. If we are not for God, we are against Him. There is no halfway; these are separate paths. It is time to start paying close attention to how we lead our lives and what our priorities are.

I was reciting the Rosary late one July evening when I

noticed the chain of my Rosary had changed to a light gold color, like the Rosaries at Medjugorje. It was made of stainless steel, and had been a silver color. I was moved. To think that I, someone who had visited hell on a regular basis, was being blessed with this occurrence was much more than I could understand. But it was clearly not my job to understand, my job was to do what God placed in my path. I continued to move in the direction I believed God wanted me to move. I continued to learn, to grow, to trust and believe that what I was experiencing was real. My gratitude knew no bounds. Only God knows the degree of my gratitude for His gifts to me. If I were to die tomorrow, I would go willingly with only the anticipation of God's goodness. I was ever-thankful and expressed this often throughout my day to God in prayer. I felt very blessed for having such a powerful piece of evidence given to me by God. My Rosary became my most treasured material possession.

In July I contacted a publisher who was interested in my story. Ed had suggested I show some of my poems to a gentleman who lived a spirit-filled life, who had access to the public through his radio stations in St. Cloud, Minnesota. He is involved in spreading the word of God. His name is Andy Hilger and he sent me to Jim Blommer, the gentleman who owns the company who printed this book. When I met with Jim Blommer, he asked if I had written a book about my experiences. I told him I had started the book, but that I was only about halfway through my story. He asked that I complete it and show it to him when I was done with it. I saw how much I had grown as I read what I had written a year before. I realized I would have to re-do the book again from the beginning, because in that preceding year, I had changed and matured to such an extent, my previous writing was like that of a child. I saw how I had been "prepared" for what was to come. I began my story again, supplemented with all I had learned from God in the interim. I saw how I was walking on more solid ground. I had needed time to understand my experiences before I shared them with others. I understood what I needed to do; and if I paid attention, my path appeared very clear.

The Secret

I struggle to stay on course;
I have a tendency to roam.
I must constantly remember,
I am miles away from home.

Deep within my memories,
hidden in my soul,
God has placed a secret,
a secret of the old.

I was just the question,
searching for my answer;
I was just the singer,
I could have been the dancer.

All along the path I took
there were signs to keep away;
I lingered there a bit too long
and almost had to stay.

Then took place a miracle,
a shedding of the old,
an act of grace, a touch of love,
more valuable than gold.

I was just a flower
searching for my garden,
instead I found a heaven
and a God who gave me pardon.

I was once a thought
looking for a mind,
now I am the light
looking for the blind.

I was shown the treasure
by the glow of love from God,
and heard promises from angels
with a smile and a nod.

I was told of times of old
when we would always win;
now I am told, "Wait patiently,
it will happen once again."

In July, 1994, Charlie, one of my best friends, died. He was the person I grew up with, the person whose parents had taken me into their home when I had nowhere else to go. He was also the person I injected drugs with. He was the friend who was there when I got out of prison after two years. He was the person I put in charge of my pre-school during the years that it operated. He was the fellow who aced the child development exams, the most gifted man I knew intellectually, when he was straight and sober. He was the man with whom I spent several summers fishing on the northern lakes of Minnesota. He was the friend I watched struggling with his addictions just as I did. He died at 43. He had struggled more desperately than anyone else I know to overcome his addiction to alcohol and drugs. He had sought help through treatment for his addictions over ten times.

The last time he went through treatment, he went home to join a woman and her son who loved him very much. He had been sober six months. I do not recall a time when he had more hope and zest for life. He was prepared to settle down with a family and maintain his sobriety. He had been on a search for God all his life, and was deeply spiritual in spite of his problems. He died unexpectedly; his death was not alcohol-related.

This man was the spark for the fire; his potential exceeded that of all the other people I had known in my life. Anyone who had contact with this man will remember him; he was that unique. I could not understand why he had died at that time, a time when things were brighter than they had ever been for him, and at the same age I was when God's grace intervened to spare me. His father had died only a few months before, and Charlie joined him on the stairway to Heaven. I will never forget him. He was one of the kindest and gentlest people I have ever known. The fact that he died straight and sober, on his way to God, makes me think he arrived there safely.

As I worked on the book throughout the summer, and into the fall, I encountered an unusually large number of obstacles. At times, it seemed like there was someone or something that did not want me to finish this book. When these things occurred, I prayed about them, whether or not I was in the mood. During the frustrating times, people generally give up, get angry, curse their fate, and blame everyone else for what is going wrong. It helped to have spiritual understanding as my frustration grew. For instance, I had completed enough of the book that I felt I should try to find someone who was competent to edit the manuscript. First, I approached someone who was extremely experienced in that area. But when I got back a portion, I found a number of errors, which was very uncharacteristic of this individual. I then called someone else I knew, but we could not come to a financial agreement. I admit to being somewhat disillusioned after these two failures to find someone to help me with the book.

As I thought about it, I came to see what I had been looking for was someone who would, in effect, complete the book for me. I was looking for someone to relieve me of my responsibility. When I realized my motive, I got down in prayer and told God I would assume my responsibility for the book, but I really needed someone that knew how to type and had a basic knowledge of grammar and punctuation. Although I had been writing for years, most of what I had written had been poetry. One hour and forty five minutes later, one of my past friends called me just to say hello. It seemed that she too had changed the focus of her life. She was now enrolled in business college and very close to graduation. She typed 93 words-per-minute and had a computer in her home. When I told her of my dilemma, she immediately volunteered to type the manuscript for me.

I explained my shortage of cash to her, explaining she would have to wait for payment until my financial situation improved. This woman, who had only known me from the bars and who had only seen my negative components said, "Don't worry about the money. I know you will take care of me; pay me when you can." Not only had she taken the book sight-unseen, not knowing if it was a worthwhile project, but in addition to her schooling, she had a part-time job and two children, and she was a single parent.

Where did her confidence in me come from? And why had she called when she did? I hadn't seen or talked to her in over a year. This is an example of the coincidences that were continually active in my life after my commitment to God. I was given obstacles. I learned from those obstacles, and then they went away. This routine happened time after time. My prayers were answered each and every time I prayed—if my motivation and understanding were correct.

> ### AA STEP 12
> Having had a spiritual awakening as the result of these steps, we tried to carry this message to alcoholics, and to practice these principles in all our affairs.

Throughout my experiences, others asked me to share my story at AA meetings, church youth groups, prayer groups and even with individuals in distress who "just happened" to be in the midst of a crisis. And although I felt very uncomfortable getting up in front of people, I welcomed the opportunity to speak to others. I believe it was something God wanted of me and no matter how uncomfortable I felt with "my assignment," I moved forward, trusting God. Each and every time I spoke to people, I learned a little more about what I was to say, and how to say it. I was very aware of the growth that was taking place in me as I moved toward God. He was giving me confidence in myself, a quality which had not been present in my life before. This confidence was a direct result of my confidence *in God.*

During the period of time when I began "receiving" longer poetry, I prayed that I would be able to share my experiences with children, being very much aware of their needs. About a week later, I began receiving poetry at that level; very beautiful words that children could understand. The following is one of my favorites:

A Child's Plea

When I was very small
and had just begun to walk,
I had an angel for a friend
and we would sit and talk.

I told no one about my friend,
for no one else could see,
the angel who was at my side
was only there for me.

We had adventures I won't forget,
special places we would roam,
yet all the time remembering
I had to go back home.

She told me of a place called Heaven,
so big you could not measure,
as beautiful as a garden,
but hidden like a treasure.

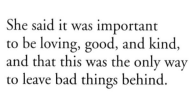

It seemed the only way to go
to this place and stay,
was to trust and to believe in God
and not forget to pray.

She said it was important
to be loving, good, and kind,
and that this was the only way
to leave bad things behind.

She said as we got older
some of us forgot,
about the angels that were with us
and how we used to talk.

She told me all about our God
filled with love for me,
and how if I did not pray
God could not stay with me.

So now I'm almost grown real big,
next week I will be seven,
and every day I pray to God
because I want to go to Heaven.

I only wish that everyone could see
how pretty it would be,
if everyone would pray to God
every day like me.

I would love to take the credit for creating that poem, but all I can honestly say about it was that it was given to me. I only wrote it down on paper. It was such a wonderful feeling to be in contemplative prayer in the evenings with only the glow of candles to light the room and receive these beautiful words. I was drawn further into the mystery of God.

I absolutely loved what was happening to me. Some people refer to the experiences that I had as "automatic writing." All I knew for sure was that it was beautiful and was filled with goodness, two very special qualities. Everything I have experienced has been filled with love and goodness. I could not deny the presence of God in all that happened to me.

In September I began to have the sensation of having my forehead touched at different times of the day. I always made the sign of the cross before prayer and it seemed as if I was being directed to pray about certain things at certain times. It was not an imaginary feeling; it was a very distinct touch. I took it to mean that I should pray throughout the day. So, all my "empty spots" became filled with prayer. I was becoming more and more focused as a result of these experiences. I was drawn ever nearer to our Lord. At times, I still found it difficult to believe these things were really happening. The question of "*why me?*" continued to move through my mind. But I knew I should not waste my time asking why. If I was supposed to know, then the answer would appear.

I continued to write down the thoughts that I received in prayer. Some were geared to adults and some were on a child's level. Here is one of the children's poems I received about 3:00 a.m. one morning:

The Story of Dewitt Debear

I have a stuffed bear
who wanders when I sleep at night,
I find crumbs of food and candy bars
in the morning at first light.

Dewitt thinks he is fooling me,
he thinks that I don't know,
he pretends he doesn't know a thing,
though I watch him when he goes.

He is into most everything
from the cookies to ice cream,
I find wrappers from the candy bars,
he thinks I'm in a dream.

I asked him once a while back
if he got up and roamed at night,
he told me he'd be scared to go
anywhere there isn't light.

But I know his day is filled with prayer
all the while he is sitting there,
so I know that he is filled with light
and he can go most anywhere.

You might ask how I could know
about this bear and where he goes,
so I must tell you what I know
from my head down to my toes.

God is not just there for me,
but everything that is,
although that's just a bear to me,
God told me Dewitt was His.

I was very thankful for being given that connection to children. I know there are many people who have not allowed Christ into the lives of their children. I believe this is one of the reasons for the powerful negative attitude we see in the young people today. If their parents only knew the joy they have rejected for themselves as well as their children, they would, without question, begin to open doors so their children could sense God's love. That we should allow the most important part of our lives, our children, to grow without the benefit of the knowledge of God is beyond excuse.

The gifts of God are peace and loving assurance. What more could we desire? Do we have the right to deny access to God to others because of our own prejudice? God's effect is life-changing and promotes spiritual growth. Receiving God's nourishment is the very reason we are here. We are not living life fully or correctly without the presence of God in our lives. If we want to make an investment for our children and their future, we should get down on our knees and pray; and we should instruct them to do the same. We cannot recognize the glory of God by denying Him. We must not allow our pride to dictate our sense of direction; we will only realize the truth if we accept it into our lives. We will not know of His truth unless we reach out.

As it is written, "Ask, and it shall be given you; seek, and ye shall find; knock, and it shall be opened unto you. For everyone that asks, receives; and he who seeks, finds; and to him who knocks, it shall be opened" (Luke 11-9).

There is no doubt in my mind that I have had many encounters with angels in the past several years. Very real encounters, not just "through" my mind while I have been alone in prayer, but also on the streets and sidewalks of this world. We are not alone! I have been asked to help certain people in certain situations; and, in retrospect, I realize that my values and my growth were being tested and strengthened. I began to become a person, a new person, shaped by the miracles of God.

On Dec. 1, 1994, three years to the day after my life had been so dramatically changed, Jim told me his company had decided to publish this book—another *coincidence* from God. My faith deepened. 🙂

22

If we go deep enough
within ourselves
we will find a hidden room.
In this room
there is a lit candle.
In the midst of the flame
of that candle is God.
If we visit this room
often enough,
we are then permitted
to leave that room
with that flame
burning in our hearts.
It is then we must begin
to help others
find that room,
using the light
we have been given.

 HE OVERALL RESULT OF MAN'S JUDG-
ments does not give us a great deal of confidence
in a fulfilling future—unless God intervenes.
We are not just destroying ourselves with our
arrogance, pride, and greed; our greed is so vast
it has nearly destroyed mother earth as well. We
should hang our heads in shame rather than
congratulate ourselves for our advancement of technology; the
advancement we should have been focused on is spreading the word
of God, His love.

We have a great deal of trouble recognizing the enormity of
our errors even as they are piled in mounds around us. We live in
our own debris, piling higher and higher as we are overwhelmed
with the results of our complacency. How long will it be before we
are willing to allow God the control we are constantly fighting for?
How much must we lose? How deep must our wounds become
before we ask and allow God to heal us? Only then will this madness we have created from our own arrogance be dissolved by the
truth of God that runs through all things.

Evil utilizes our arrogance if we allow and choose to give
control to it. What we have failed to recognize is that life on earth is
a staging area for growth; a time when we should come to understand the words "compassion," "forgiveness," "humility," and
"love." If in our time here we do not learn and understand and
grow, we have rejected the gift of eternal life God has held out to
each one of us.

When our greatest desire to get closer to God becomes our
top priority, He helps us get closer to Him; that is His promise.

And unlike the human species, God keeps all of His promises. His reliability is one of the reasons we have such difficulty believing in Him: we cannot believe that anyone that full of goodness and power *exists.* We have only truly seen it evidenced in Jesus Christ— and we killed Him!

How long are we going to continue in our arrogance? We are so blind, we deny the depth of our own ignorance. Look around you: how can anyone not be stunned by the degree to which we have destroyed ourselves and our planet? *And we still "insist" we know what we are doing!*

Ignorance is only an excuse while it applies; once we know the truth about a particular thing, yet continue to function as if we were still ignorant, that is sin. My ignorance is gone only in the realization and acceptance of God.

The most miserable and destructive advice comes to us through our ego, through which Satan operates. The influence of Satan causes us to get angry with others because of our own impatience. We then get angry at ourselves for abusing others; then, we do stupid, unloving things that we ultimately regret. We must not allow Satan to rule our lives in this way. We should belong only to the Lord. In a life filled with the Spirit of God, God is our master and there is no room for Satan's selfishness, jealousy, arrogance, or his need to win. We must realize we can only win through the mercy and love of Christ.

We should also realize that if we follow God's path, yet lack confidence in ourselves, we lack confidence in the power of God. Wisdom is not measured in years, but in the demonstration of God's principles. And just because we have let God down does not mean God will let us down. Through Jesus Christ we are forgiven; we can start anew. A new beginning is God's gift to us.

The only thing worth striving for here on earth is a loving relationship with God, for without that we have nothing. The only thing worth dying for on this earth is a closer union with God, and all goodness brings us nearer to God. With God in our lives, our boundaries move outward until they suddenly disappear in the light we receive.

We have boundaries set in our imagination that prevent us from seeing and experiencing the truth. They are the "human" part of us, that God inserted, forcing us, through faith, to choose what kind of journey we make in life, which also determines what our next journey will be. Believe, ask God to remove those boundaries. Through our prayer we will experience God's undeniable love. We must accept our built-in ignorance because within that acceptance we begin to recognize the truth that God makes available to us. And God will let us know how we should use our individual gifts in a responsible and effective manner.

If we can come to view obstacles in our lives as opportunities from God for growth, we begin to understand what this word "love" means. What may appear to others as a loss, may in fact be a win, because a loss utilized correctly reverts to a win. The correct attitude, then, is a no-lose situation. It can be called "faith" without contradiction, for, through our faith and confidence in God, we receive the courage to remain faithful.

God rewards our first step by helping us to take the next step. Growth is a progressive state, a never-ending experience not unlike our progression in school from kindergarten through graduation.

I believe this place, earth, is our beginning. That would account for our vast ignorance and arrogance, and our continuing error that is evident in a glance at a newspaper or the evening news. There are always more mistakes in the beginning of a process. Later, when we begin to understand the concepts, we become better at it because of our repetitious experiences, unless we are too arrogant to learn. I believe there are layers of existence which necessarily overlap to maintain and encourage progress. I believe we are on the first level. If we think of it this way, our perception changes; our pride is replaced by humility, because we begin to realize our knowledge is very limited. Life on earth is without question a learning experience. In some ways, it becomes more difficult as we grow in the knowledge of God, because we then become more and more aware of the error and pain which surrounds and inhabits us. We become observers of sorrows. We also see how needless this error and pain

are. If only we would turn to God for the answers instead of insist-
ing we can take our first steps alone, we would stumble less and our journey would be shortened dramatically.

> True beauty overlaps itself, extends beyond all things; it has no limits, as love has no limits.

Humility enters our lives as we begin to realize our ignorance; when our error has caused us to eliminate all of our choices one by one until we are left in the end with only the choice of God.

Without God's help, our ignorance and error are ultimately elimi-
nated by failure. Only our faith in God will shorten this potentially difficult journey. We have an advan-
tage if we receive these concepts early in our lives from parents, church, school, and healthy, loving relationships. But lacking that advantage does not mean we cannot start now by demonstrating our faith in God for others to witness, so that they might see the miracles God sends into our lives, and come to love and trust God also.

With our life on earth, God has given us the opportunity to make choices. He has given us free choice, our will. Within this will we have access to God, and we have access to Satan. We choose whom we wish to be in charge of our lives.

There is no argument against goodness, and never will be. God, the Spirit, will live on through all eternity. God, at times, chooses the most unlikely candidates to carry His message to others so that others might recognize His power, His love, and His forgiveness.

The path to God is one of growth, and growth requires change. What must change is our will; it must become God's will. God is Spirit; Satan speaks through the flesh, to tempt us. Our choice to satisfy our immediate selfish needs closes the door to God. Then we are so far away from the truth, we would fail to recognize God even if we could see Him. The *only* way to see and have the truth revealed to us is through our surrender of self (ego)

to His will. We will see *immediate* changes in our lives. That is a promise from God. We will come to recognize His Spirit in our lives. *This is the joy that Christians speak of.*

> We should thank God this is just a learning experience; that God gives us a chance to "choose" instead of just *forcing goodness* on us!

Unless we enter a dwelling, we will not know what that dwelling holds. Faith, trust, and perseverance are the key to the door of God's dwelling place. There is no other way into God's Kingdom. This is not a process of birth, life, and death; this is only the beginning. We will only achieve ultimate salvation through surrender. Surrender brings about the gift of sight we need to see the truth.

God's church can be defined as a group of people who love God more than themselves. To understand love as powerful as that, we must come to know God.

As we look at history, we see that all recognized religious leaders were headed in the same direction. Goodness was their path, and God was their motivation. When we look at how the human race has, for the most part, rejected these teachings, we see it as arrogance in action. It has become more important to be in *control* than right.

We hear and see people looking for the answers, but in our arrogance, we overlook God. It is not as though we have to rush around looking for the answers. We have been given these answers in the form of God's word and His commandments. Instead, we decide to bend God's laws just enough to make them our own. It is rather like taking a beautiful piece of art, ripping it to shreds, and then pasting it back together again with the idea that we can do it better. There are two words which describe that particular behavior: ignorance and arrogance.

We cannot be lifted up, until we have learned to bow down. The answers are all there for us, in addition to all the tools to reach God. Our attendance at church, Bible study, and our prayers hold all the answers to the questions we ask. Through prayer, God begins to give us pieces of the puzzle we call life. Through our faith, each moment, each thought, each act brings us another piece of the puzzle until we begin to see the complete picture. It only remains a puzzle until the pieces are assembled. But we are very proud and misguided. We refuse to submit, to surrender to God. We have that tendency to be imperfect; and evil can inhabit that imperfect part of us if we are not conscious of God's love for us.

Jesus has not stopped bleeding from His wounds; we continue to crucify Him every day of our lives through our selfish actions. People who have not asked God to come into their hearts supply a never-ending source of arrogance that creates havoc in our world. Our relationship with God begins within ourselves, not simply by attending church once a week. God does psychological make-overs as we surrender our will to His own. Humility is the action of asking God to replace our will with His.

As we make these changes, we will sense we have entered a corridor of love. To live inside the truth of God, to know that love and to know that no limits exist except those walls we build around ourselves, is to know Heaven on earth. The truth is only recognized through faith—so simple an instruction, so difficult a task. But God gave us instructions to live by, a path to be followed, though narrow and long.

> My purpose is to take care of the things that God puts in my path, not unlike your own.

If you believe me and change your life, even if what I am telling you is a lie (it isn't!), what have you lost by living a life filled with love?

This is not make-believe. This is

not a fantasy; it is the very reason we are here. When we approach God with trust, devotion, allegiance, and love, we are given access to God through the Holy Spirit. The Holy Spirit moves as love on the wind, it fills our sails and propels us forward toward God. Once we have experienced earth, it is difficult to imagine Heaven. But try for a moment, try to imagine no fear, no pain, no anger, no loneliness, no hunger, no disease, and no death; this beauty is what awaits you if you choose to follow the path of God.

I am truly unworthy of this wonderful mercy God has shown me. I was the lost lamb God went looking for; He found me. I did not merely change; I was made anew. God will find you if you ask. Please believe this love is real; it continues forever, and we are all part of it.

If we want to grow, we must follow our Father in heaven by demonstrating the value and realities of His wisdom. We are His children; it is our duty to obey. We are being held back by our arrogance, fear and pride—all negative thoughts. We must stop being too proud to learn!

Some people are embarrassed if God enters into the discussion. If you are such a person, answer this question: What is embarrassing about endorsing, teaching, and demonstrating acts of love, kindness, humility, patience, and honesty? Where is the shame in that? These are qualities of God, Who is very real—they should be shared. Would we want any less for our own children?

What is embarrassing and shameful is that, for the most part, we are not listening to our Father. Instead, we are listening to our fears, fears that are put there by the evil that is *real* and *powerful*, and in this fear we become confused. In the midst of this confusion, our greed, selfishness, lust, and our conflicts grow—not the type of growth God desires for us.

What is happening in this world now, through the Spirit of God, is real—and, I believe, forthcoming. I can see no other reason for the consistencies of the stories of spiritual growth and experiences shared daily throughout the world.

I was touched and moved with such intensity; I cannot ignore the timing. There would never have been a more appropriate time for this awakening to happen to me. It is, without question, out-of-character for the "old Tom" to reappear. God willing, *he* won't happen again. I believe also, there will be others who won't believe I wrote this book, that I am incapable of such an endeavor. And the truth is: I am not capable! Therein lies the power of God, to build our faith.

God, in effect, forced me to be aware of the reality of Himself. Then it was for me to make a choice—an easy choice, since I had spent most of my life in hell and, as the saying goes, I was hungry. As I became more and more aware of my path to God, I learned, through prayer, to remove the underbrush that for years had held me back. My path became evident: I was given a compass—the word of God. If I were to leave this path now, it would be no one's fault but mine. And although I still come to a place, now and then, where a tree blocks my path, I have found that prayer removes all obstacles that hinder my progress to God. And just because I may hesitate for a moment or two at that obstacle, I haven't stopped or quit or given up. I merely ask God to tell me when and how I can continue; to tell me I have learned enough about that broken tree—and then I watch as He removes it. *This is the power of God's love.*

It is not my task to make you believe what you have read in this book. I can only tell you what happened, and is continuing to happen. I will tell you one thing, though: Something extremely powerful hit me and began to work miracles in that thing I used to call "my life." What you call it doesn't matter. But, if "by their fruits you shall know them"—then know this: I call this LOVE. I call this GOD—and I call this REAL.

Pray for the courage of Christ and an endless capacity to love. This book is my small contribution in gratitude to God for all He has given me. I pray that it has helped you to recognize God's will in your life.

Remember this: God has a plan for your life, and there is no stopping it. *And all you have to do is ask!* 🖼

The truth spoken in a whisper
is still the truth,
as love gently given
remains love forever.